Convergences

INVENTORIES OF THE PRESENT

Edward W. Said, General Editor

POETRY AND PRAGMATISM

Richard Poirier

for Clifford —
best regards —
Dick 9/15/92

Harvard University Press

Cambridge, Massachusetts

1992

"Essential Oils—are wrung—" and selection from "Those—dying then" reprinted by permission of the publishers and the Trustees of Amherst College from *The Poems of Emily Dickinson*, Thomas H. Johnson, ed. Copyright 1951, © 1955, 1979, 1983 by the President and Fellows of Harvard College.

"For Once, Then, Something" from *The Poetry of Robert Frost*, edited by Edward Connery Lathem. Copyright 1923, © 1969 by Holt, Rinehart and Winston. Copyright 1951 by Robert Frost. Reprinted by permission of Henry Holt and Company, Inc.

Selection from "The Rock" ("Seventy Years Later") from *The Collected Poems of Wallace Stevens* by Wallace Stevens. Copyright 1954 by Wallace Stevens. Reprinted by permission of Alfred A. Knopf, Inc.

This book is printed on acid-free paper, and its binding materials have been chosen for strength and durability.

Library of Congress Cataloging-in-Publication Data
    Poirier, Richard.
        Poetry and pragmatism / Richard Poirier.
            p.   cm.—(Convergences)
        Includes bibliographical references and index.
        ISBN 0-674-67990-3 (alk. paper)
            1. American poetry—20th century—History and criticism.
        2. Emerson, Ralph Waldo, 1803–1882—Influence.   3. James, William,
        1842–1910—Influence.   4. Pragmatism in literature.   I. Title.
        II. Series: Convergences (Cambridge, Mass.)
        PS310.P66P6   1992
        811'.5209—dc20   91-27394
                            CIP

To Leo Bersani

Contents

Poetry and Pragmatism

INTRODUCTION

This book was written as a result of invitations to deliver two different series of lectures: The T. S. Eliot Memorial Lectures at the University of Kent at Canterbury in 1991, and, in 1990, the Christian Gauss Seminars in Criticism at Princeton University. In some cases, the chapters printed here are as much as twice the size of the corresponding lectures, trimmed as each of these had to be to an allotted time of sixty minutes, but the writing throughout was meant for the ear, each to be heard at a sitting, and I hope they retain that quality. It is an especially appropriate one, as it turns out, for the writers with whom I am principally concerned: Emerson, William James, Robert Frost, Gertrude Stein, and Wallace Stevens. However different any one of these may be from the others, all of them mythologized and explored the virtues of a public poetry and a public philosophy, all wrote some of their work as public lectures, and most of them, Stevens less than the others, coveted the idea of popularity with a general audience.

And yet, one of the complications of literary and cultural history which this book investigates is that the democratic impulse shared by Emersonian pragmatists also involved a recognition that language, if it is to represent the flow of individual experience, ceases to be an instrument of clarification or of clarity and, instead, becomes the instrument of a saving uncertainty and vagueness. As a result, my contingent of writers is perhaps finally less easy to understand, and less readily available to the culture each of them has helped bring into existence, than are poets and philosophers who write with literary and professional coteries in mind or who aspire, as Eliot thought the modernist writer should, to be "difficult." While I therefore cannot assume that these chapters will prove as easy of access as I have tried to make them, they are in tone, pace, and vocabulary intended for readers who themselves seldom make use of theoretical terminologies, who are hospitable to exploratory and digressive movements in an argument, and who might be grateful, now and then, for a few clarifying repetitions, especially when these allow some modification of a point already made or the reinterpretation of a passage already discussed.

On the subject of pragmatism, this is not meant to be in any way an exhaustive inquiry. It is partial, at once limited and somewhat biased, especially in focusing on pragmatism as a form of linguistic skepticism, and in arguing that this skepticism is equally at work, and is indeed a generative principle, in the poets I discuss. No adequately full study of pragmatism exists in any case; there are as many pragmatisms as there are pragmatist philosophers, just as surely as there are many different kinds of Emersonians, often at odds with one another. William James, in a lecture called "Philosophical Conceptions and Practical Results," delivered at the University of California at Berkeley in 1898, is credited with launching the philosophical movement called "pragmatism," but the man to whom he gives credit for inventing the term, Charles Sanders Peirce, was sufficiently annoyed with the adaptations of his friend and benefactor that he complained in a letter to Mrs. Ladd-Franklin in 1905 that "Although James calls himself a pragmatist, and no doubt derived his ideas on the subject from me, yet there is a most essential difference between his pragmatism and mine." That same year, in the journal *Monist*, he sounds even more agitated about what he regards as the widespread misuse of the term: "So then, the writer, finding his bantling 'pragmatism' so promoted, feels that it is time to kiss his child good-by and relinquish it to its higher destiny; while to serve the precise purpose of expressing the original definition, he begs to announce the birth of the word 'pragmaticism,' which is ugly enough to be safe from kidnappers."[1]

My emphasis, next in importance to Emerson, is on James rather than on Peirce or John Dewey, because James is the point of transmission, linking Emerson to Frost, Stein, and Stevens, who attended Harvard, as did Eliot in his freshman year, while James was a renowned and popular teacher in its philosophy department. It is through James that one can most profitably trace an Emersonian linguistic skepticism that, in my view, significantly shapes those aspects of pragmatism which get expressed in the work of these great twentieth-century figures. Together, they share in a liberating and creative suspicion as to the dependability of words and syntax, especially as it relates to matters of belief, including belief in the drift of one's feelings and impressions. Within this configuration I hope to reveal a line of force in literary and critical practice that has not been made visible, at least to a point of being by now a factor in cultural and literary, not to mention philosophical, narratives of development. The line from Emerson to James has itself been allowed to remain so obscure that it has had relatively little impact on the reading of Frost or Stevens, and is only beginning to be felt significantly in studies of Stein.

Emerson's contribution to American philosophy, much less to poetry and to literary and linguistic theory, has been scandalously neglected; so, for that matter, has James's. Emerson is the preeminent figure in all this, and I will keep coming back to him both to correct an injustice and because I continue to marvel at his genius. He is the inspiration for the kind of criticism practiced in these lectures and that will, I hope, come to be practiced beyond them with some frequency, a kind of criticism that might show literary and cultural studies how it is possible to move ahead of their current tedium, rancor, confusion, and professionalist over-determination. The many exceptionally able interpretations of Emerson produced over the past few decades have consisted for the most part of explications of his essays and poems and have tended to shy away from the effort to show how powerful Emerson's impingement could be on the larger cultural, social, and critical issues with which I here involve him and his successors.

This introduction is an attempt at a preliminary inquiry into the contributions Emerson has always been ready to make to cultural work, and this involves asking why that contribution has so often been ignored, or misunderstood out of critical ineptitude, or blocked out of fear. Let me begin with the example of a lengthy and admiring essay on Emerson published in 1898 by John Jay Chapman. Chapman was himself an Emersonian individualist and dissenter, a friend of William James and of other Boston intellectuals, and a man of many talents, as a lawyer, reformer, poet, essayist, translator, playwright, and resolute critic of America up to his death, at seventy-one, in 1933. His essay on Emerson remains one of the most discerning ever written, and such strictures as he allows himself merit the historical allowance given to Samuel Johnson's *Preface to Shakespeare* in 1765. We should understand that in order to persuade doubters that Shakespeare, as Johnson says, is "the great sublunary genius" or that Emerson, according to Chapman, "stands over his age like a colossus," it was necessary to deal with criticisms which were known to be retarded even at the time. Johnson set about to explain, for example, why Shakespeare had a right to violate the unities; Chapman, why it was pardonable for Emerson to scant relations between the sexes.

Indeed, it is Chapman's quite charming, brief, and innocuous comment on this alleged deficiency that is invariably singled out by later critics who like to quote it as a definitive judgment, the more so, apparently, because it is so casually derisive: "If an inhabitant of another planet should visit the earth, he would receive, on the whole, a truer notion of human life by attending an Italian opera than he would by reading Emerson's volumes. He would learn from the Italian opera that there are two sexes; and this, after all, is probably the fact with which the education of such a stranger ought to begin."[2] Close to a hundred years later, and nothing learned in the meantime, the American educated public, through some of its esteemed universities, still lends a tolerant ear to equivalent patronizations, as when, during the Massey Lectures delivered at Harvard and published in 1986 as *The American Newness,* Irving Howe expressed the wish that "in the Emersonian landscape there were rather more old shoes and aunts and cousins."

It is to be inferred from such comments that you read Emerson's essays, if you bother to read them at all, for the same reasons that you visit the local supermarket: to stock up on basic family needs. The essays are not to be read, that is, as a test of your adequacies or mine, which is how I read them, but only of his, even though, as John Dewey contended in his 1929 essay "Ralph Waldo Emerson," Emerson is "the one citizen of the New World fit to have his name uttered in the same breath with that of Plato." I ask you to imagine if disparagements at all similar to those I have cited—and there are many further such examples— would be tolerated by educated audiences anywhere about comparable European figures like Descartes or Goethe, Nietzsche or Heidegger.[3] Easygoing trivializations of Emerson, or outright refusals, as by Richard Rorty, to grant him any founding role whatever in the evolution of American philosophy, can be so amazingly unapologetic, so stubborn in their persistence, as to raise the larger question of just what it is in American culture—and in Emerson himself, since he helped invent that culture—that promotes the assumption that his writing, or for that matter the writings of William James or Robert Frost, do not need to be read with the discipline, with the expectation of difficulty and surprise, otherwise freely given to works not nearly as crowded with philosophical and mythological promise.

Emerson as a marvelous exuberant or Emerson as an antiquated preacher—he is in the one case denied any place in the canons of philosophy, as when Bruce Kuklick, in his influential *The Rise of American Philosophy,* brushes him off as "an amateur renegade," or, in the other case, dismissed from the literary canon by the novelist John Updike, who wonders at inordinate length, in the pages of *The New Yorker,* if there is "not something cloudy at the center of [Emerson's] reputation, something fatally faded about the works he has left us." To try to understand of what use Emerson might be to us—or, more properly, of what use we may be to him, to the criteria by which we are still measured by him—is to be confounded straight off by widely held assumptions that he is either a romantic provocateur or a failed family counselor, approved as a seer of no immediate relevance or patronized because he is oblivious to his own, much less to our, domestic or sexual arrangements. About sexual-social arrangements Emerson probably cannot be expected to make sense to generations imbued with the idea that the most important evidence that one's time on earth has been well spent is provided by public testimony to some ongoing "relationship," along with evidence that a "significant other" will legally confirm it. What, then, to make of Emerson, who writes in his Journals for January-February 1840, five years after his second marriage, to Lydia Jackson: "I marry you for better but not for *worse.* I marry impersonally."[4]

And yet, I would suppose that if Chapman's visitors from another planet hoped to arrive at some understanding of "human life," they would need to understand what Emerson means when he objects that he would only "impersonally" enter into the social contract of marriage, quite as much as they would need to understand claims to personal intimacy as laid bare in Italian opera. Not everyone will in any event be persuaded that less is to be learned even about relations between the sexes from the essay "Experience," a work of Shakespearean magnitude that is largely the subject of Chapter 1, than from *La Bohème,* a Broadway musical of its day first performed only two years before Chapman's essay was published. Perhaps it was Italian opera—it most certainly could not have been the essays of Emerson— which prompted Chapman to a horrendous act of self-mutilation in his rooms in Cambridge late one night in 1887. Guilty at having viciously caned a man who, so he imagined, had paid too much attention to Chapman's fian-cée, he held his offending left hand in the fireplace, burning it so badly that it had to be amputated.

Comments like those by Chapman, Howe, Kuklick, or Updike—and I will get to another in a moment—reveal the difficulty that Anglo-American literary culture experiences when it tries to do more than characterize, in a general way, some of the greatest writing done within it, including specifically the essays of Emerson. As Stanley Cavell has put it, expressing some exasperations similar to mine, Emerson still remains "unknown to the culture whose thinking [he] worked to found."[5] Anglo-American criticism in this century, except in rare instances—one thinks of earlier figures like Empson, Blackmur, or Burke, all highly suspect in the academy—has had little success closely monitoring the unrelenting flexibility of language to be found not only in Emerson but in Shakespeare or Wordsworth or D. H. Lawrence, a flexibility wherein meanings are emplaced only to be edged out by alternative ones, and where the human presence already implicit in the sounds of words can, through the very gestures that dissolve that presence, be refigured and affirmed. An earlier essay of mine, "Writing Off the Self,"[6] is an effort to legitimize for criticism this extremely complex process, in which the act of self-erasure, of disowning the words by which just a few seconds ago you may have identified yourself, becomes in fact, and paradoxically, an indication of selfhood.

The prospect of engaging in such a decreative/creative movement may not, to many readers, sound particularly inviting, salutary, or useful, and yet I mean to explain how, in exactly these ways, Emerson, and the pragmatist-poetic line I see deriving from him, can be most valuable to us. We are enjoined by his essays, his tryings out, to participate as readers in a recurrent discovery about the language we inherit: that by a conscious effort of linguistic skepticism it is possible to reveal, in the words and phrases we use, linguistic resources that point to something beyond skepticism, to possibilities of personal and cultural renewal. I need to insist, however, that the values to be found in a writer like Emerson and, through him, in literature generally, are wholly dissimilar from the value systems of those who nowadays belabor us for what is taken to be a general irreverence toward the past or who call for strict constructionist reading of a kind directed at the Constitution by Judge Robert Bork, or who polemicize in the pages of magazines like *Commentary, The New Criterion,* or *The American Scholar.* All of these longingly evoke a past that never existed, never *can* have existed, in large part because language, in which the past comes to us, is too agitated a medium ever to allow any such fixity of meaning or value as they are able—but only in the most abstract generalities—to conjure up. Nor does language as found in literary or philosophical or political writings ever sustain the astonishing fantasy that these are the places where redemption is available for the damages and wastes of contemporary history.[7]

Emerson shows how these illusions, along with their often pernicious social implications, can be dispelled through an intense relation to the language and to the literature of the past, a relation at once more troubled and more vital than any recommended by the monumentalists. Notoriously suspicious of the past as past, of the cultural artifact of the past, Emerson has been consistently misread as intending to dismiss it altogether. Thus, while president of Yale, A. Bartlett Giamatti could confidently tell his students and their parents that Emerson's "greatest contribution to our culture, and greatest disservice, lies in the assurances with which in subtle and obvious ways he justified jettisoning history." This, as it turns out, is more cartoon than criticism. When Emerson, in an echo of "The American Scholar," "The Divinity School Address," and "Self-Reliance," says in his Journals for August-September 1845, for example, that you are "here to become not readers of poetry but [to become] Dante, Milton, Shakespeare, Homer, Swedenborg . . . here to foresee India & Persia & Judea & Europe in the old paternal mind," he is scarcely to be understood as meaning that these things are all to be "jettisoned." Rather, he means that we must so thoroughly synchronize their internal workings with our own that any barrier between past and present becomes adventitious.

In his essay Dewey remarks, somewhat turgidly, that Emerson's "ideas are not fixed upon any Reality that is beyond or behind or in any way apart, and hence they do not have to be bent. They are versions of the Here and the Now, and flow freely. The reputed transcendental worth of an overweening Beyond and Away, Emerson, jealous for spiritual democracy, finds to be the possession of the unquestionable Present." From this perspective, it is as if the past is to be *foreseen* in the present, a present always intent, as the past was, on transforming itself into a very different and better future. This effort to remake history requires the most strenuous sort of writing/reading, of ourselves no less than of those in the past whose work we recreate by our readings of it. Since we literally make the past, it is a dereliction of duty to worship texts, monuments, and artifacts, including literature, as if these are products which only the past has produced.

Gertrude Stein, that most ingratiating of Emersonians, phrases the matter with characteristic audacity in *The Geographical History of America*:

> What is a master-piece.
> Any one that is no one is deceived because although any one can quote it no one can make use of it.
> It is not any loss to lose a master-piece.
> Every once in a while one is lost.
> I remember very well deciding not to worry even if a master-piece should get lost. Any master-piece ancient or modern because there is no such thing as ancient or modern in a master-piece how can there be when there is no time and no identity.
> And if a master-piece is lost then there is just one less to know about and as there are so few after all does it make any difference.
> Suppose you have them all or none at all.

> But nevertheless master-pieces do have to have exis-
> tence and they do each one they do although there are
> very few.
> We know very well that master-pieces have nothing
> to tell how can they when after all anything that tells
> what everyone tells tells what any one tells.
> I tell you that any soldiers at all look as soldiers are.
> Of course they do.
> Anybody too.
> And master-pieces do only master-pieces have to be
> what they tell well anybody can tell anything very well.[8]

A masterpiece or text, being a product of the human mind,
which is timeless, is part therefore of the mind's work-in-
progress. It only "tells" us what "any one tells," what you
or I could tell. Emerson contends similarly, in "Self-Reliance," that "In every work of genius we recognize our own
rejected thoughts: they come *back* to us with a certain
alienated majesty" (my emphasis).[9]

This brings us to the perhaps irresolvable and rewarding
conflict explored in Chapter 2. It is a conflict between, on
the one hand, a determination to imagine that there is some
sort of democratic-universal participation in the creation of
art, and, on the other, a recognition that there is nonetheless
a special measure of genius in those who do in fact produce
works of art. These specifically include Emerson and Stein,
the latter of whom declares herself a genius with engaging
forthrightness and frequency. One result of this conflict is
a stylistic imbalance that becomes especially evident when
the writer's rhetorical claim to ordinariness is coupled, as it
so often is, with rhetorical practices that give every indication of individual, eccentric, and unique mastery. Such

disproportions may emerge in the work of any writer, regardless of national origin or period, but they are unavoidable among the Emersonian pragmatists I am discussing. While they like to promulgate in theory, and exercise in practice, a mythology of public philosophy and public poetry, their actual writing ends up demonstrating how antithetical these can be to individual self-expression. Stylistically, their works dramatize how difficult it is to use language when, if it is to be true to oneself, it must presumably also be at odds with prevailing or accredited usages. One evidence of this problem is the effort to displace onto a general category of "work"—something that can be done by anyone—the aura and privilege traditionally ascribed to literary "texts." The inference to be drawn is that certain forms of intense labor, like apple picking, can become synonymous with literary creation. This can, I am convinced, sometimes happen, but it seems all the while obvious that literary texts, especially when they turn out to be "masterpieces"—including, again, those written by Emerson and Stein—manage to incorporate "work" in a fashion that charms and compels interest to a degree not as easily perceptible in any work, whether on paper or in a garden, done by John or Jane Doe. While any one of us may indeed "tell" what Shakespeare tells in his plays, no one is apt to be deceived as to who tells it better or more pleasurably. The human mind may always be the same, but the expressions of it that tend to excite most interest are particular, historical, individual, and eccentric.

Emerson is seldom given credit for the abundant care he takes of these issues, as in his essays on Shakespeare and Plato or in the essays "Art" and "Nature." He admits, in the last named, that we can become attached to a text—

that is, to a specific instance of work—precisely because it is an expression of the local and historical. He wishes to point out, however, that no matter how appealing the historical nature of any text, especially as it gets expressed in uses of language, historicity is itself the germ of what could become the cultural obsolescence of that text. In their tiresome injunction to "make it new," weak Emersonians fail to perceive that this is also to say that "it" will become old and will not thereby be discredited. Indeed, according to Emerson himself, nothing can even be recognized as new unless it offers in itself some hint of its obligation to the past. "No man," he says in "Art,"

> can quite emancipate himself from his age and country, or produce a model in which the education, the religion, the politics, usages, and arts, of his times shall have no share. Though he were never so original, never so wilful and fantastic, he cannot wipe out of his work every trace of the thoughts amidst which it grew. The very avoidance betrays the usage he avoids. Above his will, and out of his sight, he is necessitated, by the air he breathes, and the idea on which he and his contemporaries live and toil, to share the manner of his times, without knowing what that manner is.

To some, it will sound mystical to talk in this way about the cultural past and about distinctions among literary works, work, and texts; to others, especially those familiar with the more discriminating theories of textual scholarship, it will sound wholly reasonable. G. Thomas Tanselle, in my view the most distinguished and exacting of textual scholars, remarks, in *A Rationale of Textual Criticism,* for example, that "no text—embodied on paper or film or in memory—of a literary, musical, choreographic, or cinematic work" can in fact be fully synonymous with that work, which, besides, is not itself the same as the "work" or performative activity or thought that produced it. And, he continues, "those most emphatic in holding that the meaning of literature emerges from a knowledge of its historical context—those most likely, that is, to believe themselves scrupulous in the use of historical evidence— are in fact hindering their progress toward their goal if they do not recognize that artifacts may be less reliable witnesses to the past than their own imaginative reconstructions."[10] It bodes well for my efforts to revitalize a tradition linking Emerson to, among others, Stein, and to claim that new directions can thereby be opened up for contemporary criticism, that a textual scholar like Tanselle can be shown to be already participating in that tradition, though without claiming it as his own, and that so illustrious a cultural-literary critic as Edward Said can be credited with the Emersonian observation, in *The World, the Text, and the Critic,* that "the critic is responsible to a degree for articulating those voices dominated, displaced, or silenced by the textuality of texts." Alluding to a position of mine in *The Performing Self,* he remarks that "Texts are a system of forces institutionalized by the reigning culture at some human cost to its various components."

As Emerson would have it, every text is a reconstruction of some previous texts of work, work that itself is always, again, work-in-progress. The same work gets repeated throughout history in different texts, each being a revision of past texts to meet present needs, needs which are perceived differently by each new generation. While some of these texts or products may deserve to be called "classics," none is definitive, much less indispensable. The proposition that creation consists of repetition with a difference, of repeating in a new text work already being carried on in the texts of the past—this can be further illustrated by noting how the idea is itself repeated, out of the different texts of Emerson, not only, as we have just seen, in Stein, but in James and Dewey. In 1915, for example, Dewey, in *Democracy and Education,* attacks the tendency in education to focus on what he calls "past *products,*" instead of on "the life" which produced them. "The moving present," he writes, "includes the past on condition that it uses the past to direct its own movements." Similarly, in the chapter of *Pragmatism* called "Pragmatism and Humanism," James observes that any new additions to reality created in the present must, to be accepted as such, "build out" on what is already there, on "previous truths." As he puts it, "Man *engenders* truths upon" the world. A text, to take a clue from the word "engendering," is like a newborn baby: authored by its parents, its origins are lost, as are theirs, within untraceably ancient genetic codings. The baby derives from the intricate workings of creation; it is a copy in essential respects of all other babies, and yet it is a distinct text in itself. Because it is a copy it can be recognized and understood, and yet as to its ultimate source it carries within itself a mystery that neither we nor it can ever fully know or articulate. James writes:

> Every hour brings its new percepts, its own facts of sensation and relation, to be truly taken account of; but

the whole of our *past* dealings with such facts is already funded in the previous truths. It is therefore only the smallest and recentest fraction of the first two parts of reality [the flux of our sensations; the relations that obtain between our sensations or between their copies in our minds] that comes to us without the human touch, and that fraction has immediately to become humanized in the sense of being squared, assimilated, or in some way adapted, to the humanized mass already there. As a matter of fact we can hardly take in an impression at all, in the absence of a preconception of what impressions there may possibly be.

It would be contrary to the spirit of Emerson to complain that in these instances, Stein and Dewey and James do not bother to credit him for having already said several times over essentially what they are saying. In his first book *Nature,* in the section called "Discipline," he had observed, for instance, that "This use of the world includes the preceding uses, as parts of itself"; and, in "Art," that "the new in art is always formed out of the old." His three inheritors are not merely repeating Emerson, who is as surely repeating someone else. Rather, they are participating in an idea shared by all of them, though expressed in each case in terms specifically appropriate to the exigencies of the writer's own conditions and cultural locality. Each is repeating; each is also original. James, Dewey, and Stein take from Emerson not simply an idea about the past but the license, the injunction, that they should make the idea, make any idea, into their own. And they do this by troping or inflecting or giving a new voice to the idea, by reshaping it, to a degree that makes any expression of gratitude to a previous text wholly unnecessary. "What is a man born for," asks Emerson in "Man the Reformer," "but to be a Re-former, a Re-maker of what man has made." To paraphrase a sentence in "Prudence," we write not only from experience but "from aspiration and antagonism," the aspiration to be new and the recognition of how difficult it is not to be old.

The past is present in each of us as a spur, an incentive to actions that, while emulating actions taken in the past by persons like ourselves, are expected also to exceed them. Necessarily, then, self-reliance in Emerson, insofar as it is insufficiently understood to refer to the assertion of one's unique personality, gives way recurrently to its opposite, to self-dissolution, to the abandonment of any already defined Self. This is a creative process made more familiar to the present century by T. S. Eliot. I refer to the oft-quoted passage in "Tradition and the Individual Talent" where in 1919 he remarks that "The progress of an artist is a continual self-sacrifice, a continual extinction of personality." Such a linking of self-extinction to artistic progress is purely Emersonian, and Eliot was either unaware of his indebtedness or, more likely, eager to forget it when in a review of the same year, entitled "American Literature," he dismisses the essays of Emerson as "already an encumbrance."[11] On the contrary, Emerson's essays everywhere assist Eliot in this, his most famous one. Thus Eliot says that the poet must "be aware that the mind of Europe—the mind of his own country" is "much more important than his own private mind." It is "a mind," he goes on, "which changes," and "this change is a development which abandons nothing *en route*." Indeed, "the most individual parts of his work may be those in which the dead poets, his ancestors, assert their immortality most vigorously."

Though Eliot is here being, or so it would appear, no more than a "re-former," a "re-maker" of the very essays he calls an "encumbrance," there are, necessarily, differences of vocabulary—Eliot's "mind of Europe" instead of Emerson's "genius" for example. On reflection, however, the differences are apt to make it all the more evident how much closer is Emerson than Eliot to those conflicted feelings about literary culture that got expressed, though never very effectively, during the turbulence of the sixties in the United States and in Europe. Emerson, that is to say, is the more radically conservative of the two. He would not choose, for one thing, ever to limit the concept of inheritable mind to Europe or to his own country. Nor would he, like Eliot, locate "tradition" so exclusively within the texts of high culture. And the writer who says at the end of "Circles" that "The way of life is wonderful: it is by abandonment," would have had trouble with the notion that "changes" or "developments" even in poetry "abandon nothing *en route.*" Being the more exacting critic, Emerson would agree with this last statement of Eliot's only if it were amended to mean that nothing is abandoned only insofar as the something that is kept has been inferred from *works,* whereas Eliot as likely intends that we should not abandon orthodoxies, or an ideal of some simultaneous order of texts and monuments.

These differences-in-similarity help explain why the most flat-minded journal of strict-constructionist criticism and cultural nostalgia calls itself *The New Criterion,* after Eliot's *Criterion,* and not after *The Dial* of Emerson and Margaret Fuller. Those who read Eliot too simply and as cultural tract, as do the editors of that journal, fail to understand how sadly his potential Emersonianism gives way to the urgency of his personal need for semblances of order and, ultimately, for the God of Anglo-Catholicism, both of which Emerson would happily have left behind. For Emerson, says Dewey, "all 'truth lies on the highway.' " He finds it, that is, in all manner of life—and not exclusively in literature—in movements, in transits, in the abandonments of order, including any "simultaneous order." More important, these efforts at abandonment are, as he continually discovers, transformed from momentarily enabling into potentially disabling structures, into what he calls, in the essay so titled, "circles."

"Circles" in Emerson are equivalent to what are now sometimes referred to as "discursive formations." Neither of these is to be confused with pacified versions that go by the name of "shared" or "communal assumptions." A "circle" or discursive formation does far more than passively reflect or represent some form of truth or knowledge presumed to be external to it. Rather, an Emersonian "circle," like a Foucauldian "discursive formation," actively creates truths and knowledge and then subtly enforces their distribution. It follows that truths and systems of knowledge are to be viewed as in themselves contingent, like other convenient fictions, and scarcely the worse, if you are an Emersonian pragmatist, for being so. It is fictions that give us hope. Among those forms of knowledge or truth created by an Emersonian "circle" is knowledge by any individual of its sense of identity or selfhood, along with the language by which that self is codified or becomes articulate. More significant still, a "circle" also determines the vocabulary by which the self learns to *resist* its own sense of identity, especially since that identity should be recognized as, in part, an imposed one. If, as Emerson complains, a "circle" inevitably tends to "solidify and hem in the life," it follows that any idea of self to which one conforms, or on which one relies, becomes constrictive, a provocation to escape, as from a prison.

I have perhaps made Emerson sound quite bleakly deterministic, and as I read his writing, early as well as late, he does take a more imperiled view of human freedom than is generally supposed. Nonetheless, there is always at work in him what he calls the soul. Thus, directly after warning about the danger inherent in circles, he insists that individuals have the freedom and power to break out of a circle: "But if the soul is quick and strong, it bursts over that boundary on all sides, and expands another orbit on the great deep, which also runs up into a high wave, with attempt again to stop and to bind. But the heart refuses to be imprisoned; in its first and narrowest pulses, it already tends outward with a vast force, and to immense and innumerable expansions."

The term "soul" is obviously central to this enraptured and dazzling passage, and to understand what Emerson means by "soul" it helps to turn to a sentence in "Self-Reliance." "This one fact the world hates," he there writes, "that the soul *becomes;* for that for ever degrades the past, turns all riches to poverty, all reputation to a shame, confounds the saint with the rogue, shoves Jesus and Judas equally aside." Even though the "soul" in "Circles" is equated with the "heart," it is not to be imagined as an entity; it is more nearly a function, and yet no determination is made as to when the function occurs or from where it emanates. The soul has no determinable there or then, no here or now; rather, as his italics insist, it only *"becomes,"* only promises to make its presence known. That is, the soul appears or occurs only as something we feel compelled to live into or to move toward *as if* it were there; it is like James's "will to believe," it hints at Stevens's "supreme fiction," which can be traced more directly, perhaps, to Santayana's *Interpretations of Poetry and Religion.* In any case for Emerson the soul always awaits us. Thus Frost is especially Emersonian at the very end of "Education by Poetry" when he speaks of "the relationship we enter into with God to believe the future in—to believe the hereafter in." We do not believe *in* any of them, including God; they must be believed *into* an always elusive existence.

There is, from Emerson, an inferable story or narrative of soul, even if it is an open-ended one. Soul repeatedly finds itself in a circle, a circle which is already one of its creations, one of its texts, one of the governing principles that it has helped bring, or is in the act of bringing, to consciousness. Each such circle takes its shape, he says, on "the great deep," which is an equivalent, as I understand it, of Emersonian mind or genius or over-soul. To break out of a circle is not to destroy it; its remnants get taken along in the swell created by actions of the soul, just as, according to James, "previous truths" get included in any engendering of new truths. However, at the very moment this expansion is occurring, the soul knows that it is creating only a new orbit or limit as it surges past and sweeps up the boundaries of an old one. This is to say that the repeated anagnorisis or recognition in the story of soul is that its progress is forever threatened by textuality, by contraction of work into a text. Thus the creative impulse which is the soul discovers in the very first stages of composition that it wants to reach out beyond any legible form, that it wants to seek the margins, to move beyond limits or fate.

Emerson is saying, then, that the soul—he could as readily have called it "desire"—establishes its presence most vividly at the very moment when we are about to extricate ourselves from any of the commitments which the soul has already made or, for that matter, is in the process of making. Soul reveals itself in those premonitory gestures or transitions by which it abandons one form or an incipient form for the always beckoning promise of another, though this "other" will also prove a limitation. Emerson says in "The American Scholar" that the "heroic mind" is perforce devoted to action, and then, in one of his most crucial, overlooked, and naggingly suggestive sentences, he briefly defines what he means by "action": "The preamble of thought, the transition through which it passes from the unconscious to the conscious, is action." While this is very cryptic indeed, it helps us better understand the enormous investment in the word everywhere in Emerson and in pragmatism generally, despite the easy recruitment of the term, by James among others, in the service of blustering athleticism and worldly enterprise.

In this, Emerson's most punctilious use of the term, "action" is meant to describe a heroic attempt to make oneself conscious of things before they go public, as it were, before they can be known publicly by virtue of having passed into language. Once they do get into language, they immediately belong in the past; they are instantly "peptonized and faked." Those two words are James's, occurring in a passage from *Pragmatism,* in the chapter called "Pragmatism and Humanism," which, as I read it, is more or less an explication of what Emerson has in mind when he talks about the actions of the soul:

> When we talk of reality 'independent' of human thinking, then, it seems a thing very hard to find. It reduces to the notion of what is just entering into experience and yet to be named, or else to some imagined aboriginal presence in experience, before any belief about the presence had arisen, before any human conception had been applied. It is what is absolutely dumb and evanescent, the merely ideal limit of our minds. We may glimpse it, but we never grasp it; what we grasp is always some substitute for it which previous human thinking has peptonized and cooked for our consumption. If so vulgar an expression were allowed us, we might say that wherever we find it, it has been already *faked*.

To say that this passage is effectively an explication of Emerson's ideas—ideas about the workings of the soul, about action, and about the difficulties of giving present life to either of these *in* language—is less an affront to James than to Emerson, who is in danger of being simplified, or of having himself immobilized, to suit the comparison. Because if in this passage James really does offer a sufficient equivalent to what Emerson is saying, then it is legitimate to ask why Emerson himself never manages to stake out his own position with equal clarity. Why is he in his writing so much more difficult and elusive? The reason, I think, is that Emerson's skepticism about language is not, as is James's, theoretical in nature. If it were theoretical he would, like James, be able to write more from a distance and hence more clearly, as if, being outside the problem, he were being asked only to sort it out. Instead, he lets his language reveal the pathos of discovering in his own sentences how words resist his efforts to represent what he believes to be the flow or stream of his own experience. Emerson in fact is not *describing* a situation in which "previous human thinking has peptonized and cooked" reality, including such reality as is just flickering across the mind. Rather, his writing *enacts* the struggles by which he tries to keep his own language from becoming "faked." His writing dramatizes his agitations when confronted with the evidence that the words he is putting down on paper, including words of resistance and dissent, are themselves products of "previous human thinking," including his own. Once said or written, his words are always *past*. More than that, fakery lurks even in the words intended to correct this situation, to reform or trope what is past. Attempts to shape reality in language may be, from a literary point of view, dazzlingly successful, but they are always to some degree a betrayal of that reality. While James can at times subscribe to this supposition, as when he says in the chapter called "The Stream of Thought" in *Principles of Psychology* that "language works against our perception of the truth," there are very few stylistic indications in his writing that he suffers for it, or that he feels it as a threat to his own stylistic self-assurance, to his way of carrying himself in the world. Emerson's heroism of mind is that he does so suffer and that he involves his readers in that suffering as if it were their own, requiring of them some of his own heroism, his own performative and expectant optimism.

Emerson is forever trying to liberate himself and his readers from the consequences of his own writing, not merely from the consequences of other people's writing. His description of the activity of the soul asks to be read as an allegory, in which the movements of the soul in its circles represent the movements of creative energy in his sentences and paragraphs. He is saying that his own acts of composition, the very efforts at non-conformity that result in his tropings of previous truths—that these fill him with apprehensions about encirclement and fixity. How is one to cope with this situation without collapsing into silence? The answer lies, I think, in the phrase "the soul *becomes*." Note that "the soul" is first named as if, with its definite article, it were an entity; note, too, that its realization as an entity is immediately and forever delayed, its presence transferred to an ever elusive future, by the word "*becomes*." The soul never "becomes" a thing or a text; it exists in the action of becoming.

"Nothing," he remarks in "Circles," "is secure but life, transition, the energizing spirit."[12] Rely, that is to say, not on anything fixed or stabilized in your vocabulary but only on the power that allows you to move away from these, movements precipitated by desire whose object is uncertain and which, if too certainly defined, could turn thinking into mere thought, activity into inertia. As a writer, much less as a person, this is for Emerson a saving principle, and it determines the disruptive energies at work in his essays, and in the compellingly enigmatic turns of his poetry. Thus, in "Self-Reliance," after some notably strong words about power as essentially a form of transition, and directly after the sentence about the soul, his expenditures of rhetoric provoke in him a derisive rejoinder, a rejection of his dependence on the phrase that serves as his title: "Why, then, do we prate of self-reliance? Inasmuch as the soul is present, there will be power not confident but agent. To talk of reliance is a poor external way of speaking. Speak rather of that which relies, because it works and is."

With its agitated substitutions of words having to do with vocal expression—"prate," "talk," "speak"—this passage, like many others in his essays, reveals a frustration with the fact that apparently any use of language may disfigure the self in the very process of expressing it. Obviously to be avoided are "external ways of speaking," speaking in obedience to easily apprehended formulae. And avoid them he does, by the calculated opacity of that final sentence: "Speak rather of that which relies because it works and is." Like the sentence in which "the soul *becomes*," this sentence is to be experienced as it is written, and not in any clarifying translation into some other syntax. The experience is of a blur in which each of the substantives momentarily stands in place of the others, bound together with them, adhering to them. ("Adhere" is one meaning of "rely," older than the more common one which, as in the phrase "rely on," suggests not adherence but dependence.) Emerson's syntax approximates that only momentary achievement of a simultaneous fusion among agent, action, and words which for him *is* the self just before its transfiguring move into another transition.

The necessary inference is that Emerson is actually opposed to individualism in the customary or social sense in which the term is most often used.[13] That is, he is opposed to the notion of the self as something put together by a person who is then required to express it and to ask others to confirm it as an identity. Similarly, he is opposed to literature conceived as a series of more or less discrete texts each holding in trust a source of wisdom not sufficiently available elsewhere. "The real value of the Iliad, or the Transfiguration," as he says in "Art," "is as signs of power; billows or ripples they are of the stream of tendency; tokens of the everlasting effort to produce, which even in its worst estate the soul betrays."

The word "betrays," as I will have reason to point out again, echoes throughout the writings of Emerson; the complexities of betrayal and abandonment are at the center of his concerns about cultural and, indeed, biological inheritance. And he seldom uses the word without allowing for its double sense. "Betray" can mean to show or reveal or discover; it can also mean close to the opposite, to deceive, to give up something or someone to an enemy. Always working inside each word, to the extent allowed by the ongoing momentum of his sentences, he characteristically declines to separate out the word's conflicting connotations. To do so would be to participate in the illusion that language is meant to clean up the messes of life. Instead, we ought to be grateful to language, as I propose in Chapter 3, for making life messier than ever, more blurred than we pretend we want it to be, but also therefore more malleable. Within even a single word, language can create that vagueness that puts us at rest inside contradictions, contradictions which, if more precisely drawn, would prove unendurable. We willingly live with the fact that by its beneficent betrayals language constantly delivers us to ourselves, and makes us known to others, within a comforting haze. Like the soul, words can reveal the parameters of fate and limitation; just as surely, they open spaces beyond these, horizons of new, barely apprehended possibility.

In assembling the tribe of Waldo for a portrait, I find honorable places for Thoreau, Dickinson, and Dewey, give prominence to Whitman and William James, and assign central positions to Frost, Stein, and Stevens. Eliot, as indicated, belongs in the portrait, though he sits so reluctantly for it that one takes the risk of treating him unfairly by putting him there; obviously William Carlos Williams belongs in it, as does, through Fenollosa, Ezra Pound, though I am content to leave their work to others who appreciate it more than I do. In my way of estimating such things, Emerson remains the greatest of his extended tribe because more than any of the others he offers himself as a truly sacrificial figure, the one who in his writing creates ever ponderable, ever enlivening, ceaselessly vibrant energies of language within which he moves as victim and victor. This, he could be saying, is how I have learned, before your very eyes, to cope with the one medium essential to the conduct of human life in culture, the medium whose invention and reinvention distinguishes us, as Kenneth Burke suggests, from other animals. Of course other animals have languages of their own, but they have not, so far as anyone can tell, evolved cultures of their own, and for the reason that their languages are biologically transmitted, and therefore do not change; the languages are not recreated by activities of the soul. They have no literary or artistic inheritance to receive or to transmit.

Emerson makes himself sometimes amazingly hard to read, hard to get close to, all the more because he finds it manifestly difficult to get close to himself, to read or understand himself. If you want to get to know him, you must stay as close as possible to the movements of his language, moment by moment, for at every moment there is movement with no place to rest; you must share, to a degree few other writers since Shakespeare have asked us to do, in his contentions with his own and therefore with our own meanings, as these pass into and then out of any particular verbal configuration. He offers one of the truest, most realistic measures in our language of just how chancy and demanding is the job of reading, a job whose requirements nonetheless can be pedagogically met, as I try to show in the last chapter. To read intently a writer as strong as Emerson is to discover evidence everywhere in his work that he means always to contend with the words by which he represents himself to himself, as much as to others.

In part because he wanted to be a great public writer, Emerson is to be thanked for making us recognize the social and not simply personal stakes in close self-reading, stakes, I take it, that each of us would just as soon evade some part of the time. He would have us ask continually the question posed at the beginning of "Experience": "Where do we find ourselves?" As I will propose, we "find ourselves," it would seem inevitably, *in* words. And yet we need not find ourselves trapped and held there by any particular text. Words have a way of opening up gaps in themselves which, like the gaps in Frost's "Mending Wall," allow two to pass abreast. It could therefore be said that a pun is the equivalent of an Emersonian marriage, two possibilities forever linked for better but not for worse, married impersonally. "Betray" is a single word, but it forever revolves on its own double meaning, revealing within itself a constantly shifting balance of gains and losses. Emerson does not show off with language, as Thoreau is so often guilty of doing, exhibiting a superiority to it, nor is he, like James, determined on lucidity. He writes always from the inside out, not from the outside in. "The only path of escape known in all the worlds of God," he says in "Worship," "is performance. You must do your work, before you shall be released."

David Bromwich has remarked in *A Choice of Inheritance,* in an essay entitled "Literary Radicalism in America," that:

> The great practical effect of Emerson's teaching was that it gave an idea of originality to a generation that included Whitman, Dickinson, Melville, along with others who seem minor talents only in that company. He accomplished this in a society where a shapeless conformity of opinion appeared to have taken hold forever. Indeed, if one tried to imagine an America free of Emerson's influence, the strictures of [Alexis de Tocqueville's] *Democracy in America* would turn into an accurate prophecy. As it is, they have come out looking *a priori* and short-sighted. Tocqueville simply did not bank on anyone like Emerson occurring.

To describe how Emerson wants us to know him, there could be no better word than "occurring," a word whose derivations allow it to mean to run toward and also to run against. It is necessary to run toward the past while running against the past, if, in Frost's Jamesian phrase, we are ever to "believe the future in." That kind of "occurring" is most traceable in Emerson and his successors, in the work they do, and ask us to carry out, *within* language. It is work that requires a skeptical excitement about the past as it still vibrates all round us in words, and it requires a determination that this inheritance of words will be transformed by our exploitations of the treasures hidden in them, before they are passed on to the generations.

I

SUPERFLUOUS EMERSON

Superfluous" and "superflu-
ity" are tricky words, compounded of literary, sexual, economic, and thus political connotations. The superfluous has
to do with excess and luxury and exuberance and uselessness
and desire, none of which are usually thought necessary to
the rational and moral conduct of life. While the word is
not customarily associated with Emerson—I know of no
one who has done more than glance at it[1]—it is, I think, a
word essential to his understanding of himself and to the
understanding he would like to anticipate from us, his
posterity. It could be construed by his detractors to mean
that he is inessential to issues of the moment, specifically
to the debate as to what, if anything, is to be gained from
the literature of the past. And yet it is on that particular
score that he proves the virtues of his superfluousness, his
determination to show that excess is more important than
necessity, energy more lasting than any meanings it may
toss out to the intellectually sedentary. He goes unrecog-
nized by today's cultural conservatives because he is too
radically conservative, and by strict constructionists—both
groups have already been identified in the Introduction—
because he is less interested in the house built by the mason,
less interested even in the the mason, than in whatever it
is that made them both. Emerson never asks us to reclaim
some heritage of civic or rational virtues as these have been

embedded, so it is assumed, in works of the past; he wants us instead to discover traces of productive energy that pass through a text or a composition or an author, pointing always beyond any one of them. "The arts, as we know them, are but initial," he says. "Our best praise is given to what they aimed and promised, not to the actual result. He has conceived meanly of the resources of man, who believes that the best age of production is past. The real value of the Iliad, or the Transfiguration, is as signs of power . . . tokens of the everlasting effort to produce, which even in the worst estate the soul betrays."

Emerson's use of the word "betrays" is a telling instance of that linguistic play or punning which everywhere in his writing precipitates mutations and superfluities of meaning, of saying by unsaying. Obviously, it means, on the one hand, "to reveal"—as the soul is revealed to some extent by its effort to represent itself in a work of art—and, on the other, to deceive or prove faithless. In both of these senses, it is linked to superfluousness, or to what he calls that "falsehood of exaggeration" which belongs to all of us. "To every creature nature added a little violence of direction in its proper path," he says in "Nature," "a shove to put it on its way; in every instance, a slight generosity, a drop too much." Nature, like the soul, is always "becoming" more than can be contained in any text it inhabits; a text can therefore reveal no more than "tokens" of creative effort, which is why the effort is spoken of as "everlasting."

In that sense, offspring of the body, like his dead son Waldo, or of his mind, like the essay "Experience," are themselves superfluous. So, too, is the person who authored them. All partake of a genius which recurrently gets expressed in an aboriginal power of troping, of turning or changing the apparently given. This genius cannot therefore ever be reduced to anything so fixed of purpose as social or economic determinants. It must already have accepted these determinants as part of its fate in any given age, an acceptance that is the precondition of its being able to trope them. Fate is always for Emerson the precondition of freedom, a notion which implies that every individual is to some degree responsible for the worst corporately done by all of us in history. There is no exoneration in Emerson; complicity is inescapable. "The habit of snake and spider," he writes in "Fate," "the snap of the tiger and other leapers and bloody jumpers, the crackle of the bones of his prey in the coil of the anaconda—these are in the system, and our habits are like theirs. You have just dined, and, however scrupulously the slaughter-house is concealed in the graceful distance of miles, there is complicity,—expensive races, —race living at the expense of race." Writing can save us from none of this; it, too, lives exorbitantly off the checkered cultural past of its language. Writing can show us, nonetheless, how instead of trying to revoke or revere or repeat the past we might, to a limited degree, renew it by troping the language, consciously or unconsciously, which is for every person, however illiterate, a shared inheritance.

Any inflection of language is thus a small gesture of freedom. It cannot accomplish wonders; it will not change the world. But it may ever so slightly make some persons *feel* like changing the world. Probably not deserving of so big a term as "subversive," which critics nowadays, including myself, use too frequently, the act of troping or inflecting language is more like a nudge. It can perhaps modify the fate which has imposed itself through language, a fate which Emerson characterizes in the essay so named as "organization tyrannizing over character." For writers truly serious about their work, "organization" or fate is encountered moment by moment in the very structures of sentences as they emerge on the page. Emersonian inheritors like William James and his student at Radcliffe Gertrude Stein discover evidences of cultural imposition in syntax. In their view, the customary structures of sentences give precedence to substantives, while transitives, including prepositions, conjunctions, and adverbs, merely speed the way toward nouns, more or less expending themselves in the process. Superfluity, itself an abstract noun, points to a human desire to go beyond these usual stopping places in sentences, these nouns, abstractions, concepts that serve the function of homes or still points, making us their dependents. Linguistic and cultural necessity require that deference be paid to these, and yet an Emersonian tries as adroitly as possible to move away from them. Emerson invites the supposition, for example, that each of his essays is about a topic—"History," "Love," "Prudence"—or about a representative man like Plato or Montaigne, though in every such case he is interested in breaking out of the titular limit or circle. His superfluousness, like Oscar Wilde's lies, is an effort to refloat the world, to make it less stationary and more transitional, to make descriptions of it correspondingly looser, less technical, more uncertain.

In these respects, as in many others, Emerson manifestly anticipates the pragmatism of William James. James nowhere adequately acknowledges his intellectual debts to "the divine Emerson," though it seems evident to me that he owed far less to Charles Peirce for inventing pragmatism as a term than to Emerson for much of pragmatism's substance. A corresponding reluctance among interpreters of pragmatism to give Emerson his due is only now being corrected by a few critics, like Cornel West, even while it persists in the close to total avoidance of Emerson in the writings of Richard Rorty, one of American pragmatism's most influential interpreters. And yet, to cite only one example, in a single paragraph concluding the sixth section of "Experience," Emerson adumbrates no less than three ideas that were to become central to James: that life is not so much present as prospective; that new ideas, to be accepted as such, must in their articulation pay deference to old beliefs or "previous truths"; and that *any* belief should be tolerated as part of what Emerson, in an italicized phrase which James could not have missed, calls *"the universal impulse to believe."* Similarly, he precedes James in associating the vague with the essential. It should be noted on that score, however, that what distinguishes James's arguments from Emerson's is that for him the association of the vague with the essential is rooted, thanks to his having been a professor of medicine and a physiological psychologist, in his conviction that there is an unbridgeable gap between the flow of bodily sensations on the one hand, and on the other the language by which we try to represent this flow. He felt most keenly the anomaly that though we cannot adequately inform ourselves through language about most of what goes on in our bodies, we presume confidently to describe what is going on in the universe.

Pragmatism, in James's version of it, is a philosophy that recommends "vagueness" as a counteraction to the dogmatizing of existent truths and as the necessary condition for the exploratory search for new truths. This search is not to be confused with a ramble. Vagueness requires a disciplined resistance to the blandishments both of conclusiveness and of common sense. For if vagueness is preferred to certainty, then it must to some extent be a determined preference. On other occasions I have pointed to evidences in James of a tension between his promotions, compounded by self-advertisement, of will and action, and the more insinuated privileges he gives, as early as *Principles of Psychology,* to receptivity and to an Emersonian abandonment of acquired selfhood, all this despite his fears of that near suicidal paralysis of purpose that he had experienced in the late 1860s.[2] Ross Posnock has very effectively demonstrated how, in fact, Henry James, Jr., dear old Harry as his older brother took to calling him, came closer to William's ideal of relaxed but vigilant receptivity than did William himself.

And yet the contradictions that can be found in William are, I suspect, more terminological than real. Just as Emerson warns that true individualism depends often on a willing suspension of self-assertion, lest in speaking your mind you inadvertently speak someone else's, so James asks us to take care lest our own cherished beliefs block or disrupt the flow of experience. In making this argument, he distinguishes "vagueness" from "waywardness," as this latter term is used in "Pragmatism's Conception of Truth" to mean willful or headstrong. He there proposes that the discovery of truth can occur with the advent of an object whose appearance was already signified or hinted at by previous experiences, but that if we too tightly control the flow of experience, if we do not remain open and flexible, then we will have missed these little pointers and therefore be unprepared to recognize the truth when it does appear. He concludes that "Truth, in these cases, meaning nothing but eventual verification, is manifestly incompatible with waywardness on our part. Woe to him whose beliefs play fast and loose with the order which realities follow in his experience; they will lead him nowhere or else make false connexions."

James here expresses a desire—that individual experience should be released from the control of any conventional or imposed or already timed narrative sequence—which he had articulated even before the publication in 1890 of *Principles of Psychology,* whose most famous chapter, "The Stream of Thought," helped name the so-called stream of consciousness techniques of twentieth century writing. Ironically, in view of James's intentions, the technique often proved to be as Draconian an imposition of technical ingenuity on the vagaries of human experience as literature has ever contrived. James would, I suspect, have been appalled by *Ulysses.* He was in no sense opposed to form. Indeed, Emersonian pragmatism is formalist in spirit in the sense that, as "Circles" makes clear, the making of form is the necessary prelude of the effort to escape its limitations. But James is opposed to the calculated superimpositions of form and to the distortions these can effect on emergent, "superfluous" materials.

The scorn expressed by Emerson in the phrase "impudent knowingness" has a corollary in James's disavowal of "common-sense categories." These can block the stream of experience no less than can willful applications to that stream of some belief or other. For while the phrase "common-sense categories" might seem to carry positive connotations for Emersonian pragmatism as it is popularly understood, James treats these categories with the skepticism Emerson himself directs at any inherited text. "Common-sense categories" are what certain geniuses discovered in the past and are now taken to be explanatory, when they are merely previous. James complains in *Pragmatism* that "The common-sense categories one and all cease to represent anything in the way of *being;* they are but sublime tricks of human thought, our ways of escaping bewilderment in the midst of sensation's irremediable flow." It is in response to this situation that he had already said in *Principles of Psychology,* "It is, in short, the re-instatement of the vague to its proper place in our mental life which I am so anxious to press on the attention."

There are etymological connections among the words "vague," "vagrancy"—a particular favorite of James's, "extravagance," and "extra-vagant," connecting them to "superfluity," and we can let Thoreau, in the conclusion to *Walden,* pull them together for us:

> It is a ridiculous demand which England and America make, that you shall speak so that they can understand you . . . I fear chiefly lest my expression may not be extra- vagant enough, may not wander far enough beyond the narrow limits of my daily experience, so as to be adequate to the truth of which I have been convinced. *Extra vagance!* it depends on how you are yarded. The migrating buffalo, which seeks new pastures in another latitude, is not extravagant like the cow which kicks over the pail, leaps the cow-yard fence, and runs after her calf, in milking time. I desire to speak somewhere *without*

bounds; like a man in a waking moment, to men in their waking moments; for I am convinced that I cannot exaggerate enough even to lay the foundation of a true expression. Who that has heard a strain of music feared then lest he should speak extravagantly any more forever? In view of the future or possible, we should live quite laxly and undefined in front, our outlines dim and misty on that side; as our shadows reveal an insensible perspiration toward the sun. The volatile truth of our words should continually betray the inadequacy of the residual statement.

There are a number of hints here of arguments I will be making. Note that Thoreau, "quite laxly," as he recommends, links true "extra-vagance" to parenting, and hence to generative sexuality, preferring, as against the migratory habits of a buffalo, the cow who runs after a calf in milking time. Note, too, that in extolling the linguistic analogues to "extra-vagance"—or superfluity or overreaching—he expects them to yield what he calls "the volatile truth of our words." In that sense, superfluity should, as James has already been heard to intimate, "continually betray the inadequacy of the residual statement." His pun on the word "betray," like Emerson's, suggests that whatever reveals a meaning can have the effect also of denying it. Here, again as in Emerson—or for that matter in Shelley[3]—extravagance is associated also with speed, with momentum or volatility of style. Extravagance in writing is more, that is, than simply a matter of the local magnification of a word. It can involve a kind of rapid or wayward movement of voice, something often heard in the casual, idiomatic passages of speech, as it simultaneously focuses on particular things and, by transition of tone or attention—by a preference for anything other than the nouns about which Gertrude Stein, as in "Poetry and Grammar," has much to say—moves away from them. Thus, as writing or speaking proceed, they can create significances, especially by inflections of voice, that "betray" the words that have just been uttered.

The implication is that there is always a signified (to evoke a later and to me not very satisfactory distinction) perpetually in want of signifiers to catch up with it, a signified (or over-soul if you will) which is always receding, drawing or provoking us, as does Cleopatra her Antony, into ever greater volatilities, meanderings, or excesses of usage. That is why Thoreau says "continually betrays," as if the tension between the revelation and denial of a meaning is a difference never to be eluded. There is in the nature of things, it seems, a conflict between signifiers and signified, or, in any metaphor, between the icon and subject. The passage from Thoreau is only inferentially about metaphor; it is, more ascertainably, a recommendation about how thinking should proceed. Obviously, however, the two—the processes of thinking and the elaboration of metaphor—are inseparable, a point left to be made not so much by William James as by an assiduous reader (and teacher) of his writings, Robert Frost, specifically in "Education by Poetry." Frost there argues, in terms very different from my paraphrase, of course, that the linguistic location or naming of a thing stimulates an instinct to take exception, to discover the insufficiency of the terms being proposed. For that reason alone any metaphor is bound eventually to break down, pointing toward and indeed requiring the invention of still other metaphors.

But the "residual statement," as the phrase implies, cannot, anymore than can the icon of a metaphor (think of Frost's apples or Thoreau's beans), be wholly dispensed with. Here, as throughout, the conservatism of Emersonian pragmatism comes into play. William James, following Emerson, maintains that in the pursuit of truth, pragmatists must always be working with previous truths. For them, a condition of thinking partakes of a condition of punning, in which gains and losses of meaning are in a continuous and generative interaction.

■

I am finding a way into Emerson's great meditation on gains and losses, his essay "Experience," published in 1844, two years after the death from scarlet fever of his beloved son Waldo, at age five. The condition which Emerson describes for himself at the beginning of that essay is of someone suffering a sense of loss without as yet any prospect of creative gain. The opening paragraph nurtures its own stylistic lassitudes with little evident hope of getting out of them; it is in the mode of Stevens when he says in "The Man Whose Pharynx Was Bad" that he is "too dumbly in my being pent" or of Frost when he says in "Desert Places" that he is "too absent-spirited to count." "Count" asks us to think of metrical feet; "dumbly," of some negating self-reflectiveness. Both poets are clearly talking, as is Emerson, about a loss of creative powers, of poetic energies and, analogously, of sexual potency. Emerson wonders:

> Did our birth fall in some fit of indigence and frugality
> in nature, that she was so sparing of her fire and so
> liberal of her earth, that it appears to us that we lack the

affirmative principle, and though we have health and reason, yet we have no superfluity of spirit for new creation? We have enough to live and bring the year about, but not an ounce to impart or to invest. Ah that our Genius were a little more of a genius! We are like millers on the lower levels of a stream, when the factories above them have exhausted the water. We too fancy that the upper people must have raised their dams.

The references to birth and to the predominance of earth over fire are delicate ways of referring to the dead son without making a monument to that loss; they also refer to the writer himself (another Waldo). The immediate off-spring of the writer Waldo is to be this essay called "Experience," this effort to discover the energy needed to pass beyond the temptation merely to monumentalize the past, and to move on to a "new creation." And yet, these conspicuous *we*'s and *us*'s refer to more than the author himself and, in the Dantean mode of the passage, to more than "we" in America. Who is this "we," already called to our attention in the initial and much pondered first sentence of the essay: "Where do we find ourselves?" Insofar as this question has to do merely with the location of "we," the answer is immediately forthcoming, for what it is worth: we find ourselves, he says, "in a series of which we do not know the extremes, and believe that it has none. We wake and find ourselves on a stair; there are stairs below us, which we seem to have ascended; there are stairs above us, many a one, which go upward and out of sight."

I have never found these sentences as affecting as they are apparently supposed to be, and far from signalling, as is often alleged, a significantly darker mood than any found in his earlier writing, they are a tepid imitation of a passage he wrote in 1841, a year before Waldo's death, for "Lecture on the Times."[4] By saying this, I mean to suggest that there is reason *not* to be reverential about the opening of "Experience," especially since he will at the end admit that this first section is written under the weight of only one of his six lords of life, "Illusion."[5] I propose that this "we," far from conjuring up some grandiose humanity, refers rather to Emerson along with his genius or muse. That is, he is struggling not with questions of human grief and inevitable loss but with his plight as a writer called upon to create an essay in the face of grief and loss. Thus the answers he does offer to the question of location—"Where do we find ourselves?"—only indicate by their very triteness that better answers must be sought. And these answers can themselves only be figurative, involving the contrivance of still other, different metaphors, perhaps no more satisfactory. Indeed, the question of the essay becomes this: how do we ever find ourselves except *in* metaphor, in the *making* of metaphor, even though the effort, as in this instance, proves unavailing? This is in essence the question at the very center of William James's pragmatism.

"Where do we find ourselves?" I have said that this "we" refers to Emerson in colloquy with his genius, and that the opening of the essay is a commiseration with his genius for their shared enervation and for their having to write under the stress of Illusion and depression. We are not coming to life, he seems to be saying, in the place where as a writer I could hope to do so, which is in the language of these sentences, and this failure could prove disastrous because the only mode of public existence shared by me with my genius *is* language, no matter how much either of us may share the illusion of unmediated expression, that genius and language or that self and language can be as one.[6] "Where do we find ourselves?" In a struggle with language—where else? In pursuing this kind of argument I have before, both in *A World Elsewhere* and in *The Performing Self,* evoked D. H. Lawrence in his foreword to *Women in Love*: "Any man of real individuality tries to know and to understand what is happening, even in himself, *as he goes along*. This struggle for verbal consciousness should not be left out in art. It is a very great part of life. It is not superimposition of a theory. It is the passionate struggle into conscious being" (my emphasis). The dramatized failure of such a struggle at the opening of "Experience" leads the voice, as it picks up a more distinctive accent, to the admission that it is in need. It is not in need of grief; it is in need of the creative energy of which grief has helped deprive it. It needs what he calls "superfluity of spirit," an infusion of power. Genius or inspiration must speak more powerfully through him if he is ever to achieve a "new creation," ever to pass beyond this tone of lassitude, with its familiar-sounding figurations.

Consider now the final comparison in the paragraph: "we are like millers on the lower levels of a stream." This comparison has been ignored by interpreters for the good reason that it sounds like simply one more effort, this time with a bit of Emersonian democratic rusticity, to respond to the question "Where do we find ourselves?" And yet if this "we" really is "like millers," why then, by adding the word "too," does he so slyly, almost surreptitiously, suggest that it is a different "we"? "We too fancy that the upper people must have raised their dams." It would seem that the persons referred to in the phrase "we too" do not usually confuse themselves with millers, with folks on lower levels of the stream. The implication is that "we" and "we too" meet at the stream much as do the farmers who work side by side with poets in Thoreau's bean field. "Some," says Thoreau, speaking in both roles, "must work in fields if only for the sake of tropes and expression." That is, Emerson's "we too" is deprived of superfluity in a poetic sense and not simply, if at all, in an economic one—as is the other "we," the ordinary laboring person. Millers worry about exhausted waters, while geniuses worry about exhausted or obstructed sources of inspiration; for millers, the "upper people" are the economically and geographically privileged; for geniuses, the "upper people" would consist of greater poets or that Divinity which Emerson has in mind when he says in the essay "Art" that "the reference to all production [is] at last to an aboriginal Power."

For reasons more fully gone into in the next chapter, it is crucial to note here that Emerson has in mind "production," whether by poets *or* by millers. That is, even while poets and millers produce different things, and even while they therefore have different needs, it is the requirement of "superfluity" which makes the poet's need as complicit as the miller's with capitalist economy—for the reason that capitalism is preeminently the economy of superfluity.

By "all production," then, Emerson means to include economic production, the production of wealth and artificial life, along with poetic production. Absolutely essential to any understanding of him, and of his differences from the ubiquitous demonizers of technology and the media in our own time, is his willing acceptance of the so-called artificial. "We talk," he says "of deviations from natural life, as if artificial life were not also natural." So that while in the shorter essay "Nature," where this sentence occurs, he allows that riches, or the "hanging gardens" of the "upper people," can create what have since been called "false needs," he himself does not find them false at all. Indeed, he wants to insist that nature in its *own* extravagance and excess creates needs that can be similarly described as "false." Nature promotes and participates—as do we all— in the temptations exuded by the productions of capitalist economy. "We heard what the rich man said, we knew of his villa, his grove, his wine, and his company, but the provocation and point of the invitation came of these beguiling stars. In their soft glances, I see what men strove to realize in some Versailles, or Paphos, or Ctesiphon." Still more pointedly, in the essay called "Wealth" in *The Conduct of Life,* he associates the esteem given to wealth with the larger desire of human beings for the "assimilation of nature to themselves," and he connects market speculation with "*speculative* genius." In both speculative ventures he discovers "a madness of few for the gain of the world. The projectors are sacrificed, but the public is the gainer."

Here again, loss and sacrifice are the condition of gain; excess and madness create, by the disappointed hopes they engender, a new equilibrium beyond the circle of the old one. In this vein, Emerson was writing a kind of *Moby-Dick* before Melville's, though in a very different key. It could also be imagined that he is writing a prelude to the essays of Georges Bataille on expenditure (collected in English in *Visions of Excess*) and to Bataille's nearly impenetrable novel *Le bleu du ciel* (*Blue of Noon,* as translated by Harry Matthews), brilliantly interpreted in Leo Bersani's *The Culture of Redemption*.

Only in such connections as these, and not with respect merely to anything so ludicrously provincial as the American market economy after the financial crisis of 1837, can Emerson's economic metaphors in "Experience," and in his other essays, be intelligently read.[7] Those who would entrap him in such local and blinkered historicist readings are described sufficiently in "Experience" itself, where he speaks disdainfully of "theoretic kidnappers and slave-drivers." He is alluding to phrenologists, of whom there are today equivalents in sufficient number within every department of literature. "The grossest ignorance," he says, "does not disgust like this impudent knowingness."

By itself the word "knowingness" is sexual enough in its connotations; and it becomes far more so when modified by the word "impudent." Now, as in Emerson's time, "impudent" means impertinent or presumptuous. Earlier it as easily meant shameless; *pudency,* meaning "modesty," is etymologically related to *pudendum.* "Impudent knowingness" is knowingness that, resentful of anything it cannot explain, presumes to expose the mysterious sources of creation, whether of human offspring like Waldo or human offspring like literature; it exposes the genitalia, as if, by pornographically pointing to this or that or any other single organ, it could explain desire or the productivity of mind. That Emerson fully intends this sense of "impudent" becomes evident several pages further on when he remarks that "the art of life has a pudency that will not be exposed."[8]

When a writer who is given to this kind of unitalicized and intricate suggestiveness also uses metaphors of a more publicly accredited kind—to return to economic ones—it is in full awareness of their drastic failure to account for life or for art. "The art of life" cannot be reduced to politics or economics or to sexuality itself, because what Bersani says of Bataille could as properly be said of Emerson: none of these things "is imagined as ever being independent of desiring energies, of a fundamentally erotic (but not necessarily specifically sexual) self-expenditure." Capitalism is, for Emerson, simply another human invention designed to satisfy the rage for the superfluous. Capitalism is one more product of the aboriginal power in which we all share, some more and some less; it is not an alien "system." As is *Hamlet* or any other text, capitalism is superfluous, while at the same time being an expression of our need for superfluousness. It is a metaphor, which like any other must, when pushed too far, break down.

Those who complain that the uprisings of the eighties in Eastern Europe were motivated less by a desire for freedom than for VCRs and Häagen-Dazs ice cream are, from an Emersonian vantage, naive. These items are evidence, however trivial, of a human need for superfluousness. It is a need anterior to ideology which can nonetheless help create an ideology of freedom. William James is thus fully Emersonian when he observes in "Reflex Action and Theism," an address to be found in *The Will to Believe,* that:

> Man's chief difference from the brutes lies in the exuberant excess of his subjective propensities—his pre-eminence over them simply and solely in the number and in the fantastic and unnecessary character of his wants, physical, moral, aesthetic, and intellectual. Had his whole life not been a quest for the superfluous, he never would have established himself as inexpugnably as he has done

in the necessary. And from the consciousness of this he should draw the lesson that his wants are to be trusted, that even when their gratification seems farthest off, the uneasiness they occasion is still the best guide of his life, and will lead him to issues entirely beyond his present powers of reckoning. Prune down his extravagance, and you undo him.

What James here sees as a human commitment to superfluity, for more than is necessary to survival—isn't it exactly this which explains both the accelerated pillage of the globe and the worried recognition that before long human beings may have left themselves irremediably destitute? If communism failed because it set itself in opposition to superfluity, so for the opposite reason may capitalism, which has greedily set out to destroy a nature that offers exemplifications of capitalism's own best practices. Nature is being deprived of its capacity to exist in a condition of excess. It was left for Melville to envision this as capitalism's destiny, murderous and self-annihilating,[9] and it is a destiny already implicit in Emerson.

"Getting and spending we lay waste our powers," as the poet says, once again suggesting the affiliation of economic and sexual enterprise. By its accelerations of a process perfectly natural in itself, the human race is destroying what has munificently been given it. It is a gift of such proportions that it complicates the instinctive impulse of Emerson to mourn for his son or himself or the future of the world. In the poignant concluding paragraphs of "Experience," he admits, "All I know is reception; I am and I have: but I do not get, and when I have fancied I had gotten anything, I found I did not." He cannot be expected to grieve for a son that was not his to begin with. This is not elaboration or posturing after the fact, designed to explain obstacles to his expression of grief; it is a position he recognized from the very start. In his Journal, dated October 31, 1836, the day after the birth of Waldo to Lidian and himself, he writes of the "Blessed child! a lovely wonder to me, and which makes the Universe look friendly to me." The intimation that the child is a gift rather than a begetting is confirmed in his adding "Otherwise I see nothing in it of mine; I am no conscious party to any feature, any function, any perfection I behold in it. I seem to be merely a brute occasion of its being & nowise attaining to the dignity even of a second cause no more than I taught it to suck the breast." Waldo belongs less to him or Lidian than to that primordial power to which, as we have heard him say, all production at last refers. It is this power which produced not only the son but Emerson himself; it produces Emerson's writing. And because he is a self-confessed genius in that writing (allowed, therefore, as in his shaded hymn to light, to evoke the divine gift of superfluity), he must also acknowledge that to some degree he participated with the Godhead in the killing of his own child.

We have just heard him affirm his own existence in the phrase "I am," a phrase recurrently used in the essays. It looks ahead to the Stevens of "It Must Give Pleasure" ("I have not but as I am, I am"), and back to Exodus, "I AM THAT I AM." This is to be kept in mind, I think, in the seventh section of "Experience," which, following his list of "the lords of life," could be entitled "Subjectiveness." It is here that Emerson's willing complicity in the worst finds itself in a gruesome pun: "The subject," meaning himself, "is the receiver of Godhead, and at every comparison must feel his being enhanced by that cryptic might."[10] "Cryptic" means mysterious—that the source of the "might" which enhances him cannot easily be located; it also means, eerily, that he shares in the hideous power of this "might" to encrypt or entomb the object. The object in this case includes both his stifled inspiration and the child buried at that moment in Dr. and Mrs. Ezra Ripley's tomb.

It should be obvious that Emerson is not writing theatrically, not dramatizing an argument already made in his head. Instead he is exploring his language as it emerges, discovering the dense and terrifying implications of his way of thinking and of his way with words. In another pun in a previous section, which, again following his list of "lords," could be called "Surprise," he had written, "We thrive by casualties. Our chief experiences have been casual." We do not, that is, need even to will the deaths of sons and lovers in order to have been complicit with them. If everything comes to us as a gift, then losses are also gifts, and he can show for the loss of Waldo this: the greatest of his essays, along with one of his best poems, "Threnody." These, too, are a gift, in part because linguistic codes are no more of his making than are genetic ones.

Emerson's faith in the power of invention is limitless; it expresses his conviction that as humans we participate in the *whole* of creation. Not only are economic systems and the plays of Shakespeare invented; so is the human mind, so is nature. Because the possibilities are infinite, any particular thing or text is in itself superfluous, part of a nearly overwhelming excess of productivity which is the essence of the universe as he conceives of it. Any one of us assists, accelerates, tropes within this flow of things, and out of the profusion one invention easily becomes the casualty of another; nothing dares risk immobility. Remarking in "The Method of Nature" that "the wholeness we admire in the order of the world" has, as he alarmingly puts it, the "smoothness of the pitch of the cataract" and that "its permanence is a perpetual inchoation," he proposes that if anything could stand still in this cataract it would be crushed, and that "if it were a mind, would be crazed." I take his comparison of the loss of Waldo to the loss of an estate as just such an effort, rhetorically, to "stand still," to deal with his feelings in an economic terminology fore-known to be pitilessly restrictive. He had in fact more right to mourn for an estate, where profit and loss do depend on controllable human actions, than to mourn the loss of a son whose birth he had already attributed to "the Cause of Causes."

The essay moves through these interwoven complica-tions of feeling with a Shakespearean refusal to sacrifice any of them to merely apparent coherence, even while "impu-dent" critics delight in contending that he is heartless or that he fails to mention the women in his household with sufficient gratitude or that he shows a refusal to mourn— a phrase much favored in recent interpretations of Emerson and Melville. But any call by a writer to the muse or to inspiration or to a God, complaining of personal deficiency at the moment of attempted composition, is a confession that a work of literature—if it is to be written—needs words in excess of the minimum daily requirements of human beings. Assuming that human beings can be called animals who use language, there are nonetheless some hu-mans who, more than others, know how to exploit its resources. The call for superfluity or, you might say, super-fluency, is compelled by a poet's recognition that language within its merely social-historical provision is insufficient when it comes to the writing of literature.

It is in the light of such traditions of invocation, of the "descendent theme," as Geoffrey Hartman calls it, that the opening of "Experience" is best understood. If its first sentence—"Where do we find ourselves?"—is a question about language, then it asks "Where do I find a language sufficient to represent the place occupied by human beings within the creation, a precious part of which, my own lineage, my future as Waldo Emerson, has just been taken from me?" As he continues, still deprived of the help he calls for, he sarcastically questions the capacity of Genius, his partner, to assist him: "Ah, that our Genius were a little more of a genius." Not being able to summon Genius into himself, he is earthbound, so to speak, by a language provided by the market, by what Bataille, among others, calls a "restricted" as against a "general economy." Emerson is not at all scornful of such market language; and there is no reason why the reader should be or why it should be treated as necessarily corrupt or corrupting; it is scarcely cruder, for example, than the Freudian jargon of id, ego, and superego. Emerson had already admitted, seven years earlier in "The American Scholar," that no artist can "entirely exclude the conventional, the local, the perishable from his book, or write a book of pure thought, that shall be as efficient, in all respects, to a remote posterity, as to contemporaries, or rather to the second age. Each age, it is found, must write its own books; or rather each generation for the next succeeding. The books of an older period will not fit this."

It is evident throughout Emerson's Journals and correspondence that he doted on his son. In "Threnody" he refers to him as "the hyacinthine boy," a reference less to the flower as we know it than to its source, said to have been the blood of Hyacinthus, the boy beloved of Apollo but killed by Apollo's own discus, thrown in play and blown fatally off course by the jealous Zephyrus. This allusion beautifully elaborates Emerson's sense that he was so far from having a merely conventional relation to the birth of his son that he must, like Apollo the god of poetry, be obliquely responsible for his death. His attachment to the Waldo of flesh and blood is displaced here, as in the Journal entry about his birth, from familial to literary-mythological offspring, which may excuse him, incidentally, for omitting Lidian, the boy's mother, from his meditation.[11]

It follows that he should throughout the essay envision his posterity as literary rather than as biological; his offspring are future readers and writers. This is where Whitman and Hart Crane, his literary sons, themselves childless, will also look for descendants. No matter how much, in the creation of his sentences, he must involve himself, as he did in the brute creation of Waldo, with "the conventional, the local, the perishable," he desperately needs that plentitude and power of language that may propel his voice into the future, just as it has carried to him the sounds of the great writers of the past whom he now echoes. A passage previously discussed, which occurs in the Journals for August-September 1845, might accordingly be re-phrased: "You are . . . here to know the awful secret of genius, here to become not readers of poetry but Dante, Milton, Shakespeare, Homer, Swedenborg"—and Emerson. This addition only confirms implications already there;

Emerson's references to "you," like those in Gertrude Stein, are very often ways of addressing himself, as to what he should or would ideally "become." The heritage most worth reclaiming consists of exemplifications of energy and fullness always and forever available *in* yourself; its merely textual embodiments, however admirable, are also superfluous.

I am still in the process of explaining, among other things, why Emerson's metaphors of market, usually read as examples of his deficiency of feeling or grief for the death of Waldo, ask instead to be read as expressions of literary pathos for the possible death of that superfluity necessary to all great writing and to life itself. The passage in question follows:

> In the death of my son, now more than two years ago, I seem to have lost a beautiful estate,—no more. I cannot get it nearer to me. If tomorrow I should be informed of the bankruptcy of my principal debtors, the loss of my property would be a great inconvenience to me, perhaps, for many years; but it would leave me as it found me,—neither better nor worse. So is it with this calamity: it does not touch me: some thing which I fancied was a part of me, which could not be torn away without tearing me, nor enlarged without enriching me, falls off from me, and leaves no scar. It was caducous. I grieve that grief can teach me nothing, nor carry me one step into real nature.

It can of course be said, and therefore repeatedly has been, that these comparisons are "shocking" or "heartless" or "cold" or "confusing." It could also be said that King Lear had a bad temper, or that one cannot admire Michelangelo's great reclining figures of Day, Night, Evening, and Dawn, because, as Constance Fenimore Woolson once complained to Henry James, "They looked so distracted." His rejoinder, as she herself had the good humor to report, was "Ah yes, *distracted*. But then!"[12]

"Ah yes. Emerson in 'Experience' does not *grieve*. But then!" In fact, however, he is not here admitting that he does not or cannot grieve. Rather, as in some sentences just before those I have quoted, he is saying that grief itself is "shallow" and that it only plays about "the surface." It is the case, as we shall see, that there is for Emerson nothing behind the surface anyway. He says that "grief has taught me nothing," and it must be wondered why he allows the inference that he had anything to learn from it anyway. Most significantly, I think, he says the calamity "doesn't touch me" and that "I cannot get it nearer to me." These are figures of touch and of drawing something toward you, and they anticipate a pun later on when he refers to "the unhandsome part of our condition." Such complaints relate inescapably to his own writing, about its failure so far to deliver into his hand, literally into his writing hand, the true significance of the "calamity." By contaminating his language with economic metaphors so evidently in vogue, he effectively reproduces the shallowness that under any circumstance belongs, he says, to grief. In the Journals for 1838, Emerson speaks of his close study of Ben Jonson, a Renaissance poet scarcely insensitive to the possible diminishments that accompany any equation of economic profit and loss with human generative possibilities. Emerson would have known, that is, how in a different historical era it was possible to write an affecting poem in which grief for the loss of a firstborn son is talked about as if the son were a loan that must be paid ("Seven years thou wert lent to me, and I thee pay, / Exacted by thy fate, on the just day.") Of all writers, Emerson would never suppose that metaphors which served well enough in a past century, where capitalism was emergent, could just as comfortably be put to use in his own, where capitalism had become rampant.

This perceived inadequacy of the metaphors he finds himself using is exactly what prompts his complaint, voiced a few paragraphs earlier, that he has "no superfluity of spirit for new creation."[13] However, directly after the passage on grief and economy, and bringing the section on "Illusion" to a close, there are, in the pun on "unhandsome," some at least incipient evidences of an infusion of superfluity. It is a pun that eagerly asks to be noticed, as does the accompanying admission that he is still looking for a grasp or hold on language that might bring reality "closer to me." "I take this evanescence and lubricity of all objects," he writes, "which lets them slip through our fingers then when we clutch hardest, to be the most unhandsome part of our condition." There are, as we have already seen, more "handsome" or hands-on puns to come. Puns hold us to a double meaning, each side of which salvages the other at the very instant when one or the other seems about to be lost. The word *Waldo,* while never appearing in the essay, can be thought of as a pun, in that the lost Waldo secures himself in the survivor of the same name only on condition that they will together share a joint posterity, less in grief or memory or monument than in the very activity of writing now going on in the essay. The son becomes the father's precursor.

Having quoted the pragmatist James on superfluity in

relation to capitalism, I will now quote the poet Frost (a declared admirer of Emerson, no less than of James) on superfluity in relation specifically to style. As Frost would have it, man writing is also "man thinking," Emerson's phrase to describe the hero of "The American Scholar." Thinking/writing is different from thought/texts; thinking/ writing shapes itself as an action that tropes rather than reveres or mourns the creations of the past. The passage, which comes from a letter to Louis Untermeyer in 1924, gives clear evidence that Frost is exactly recalling the phrasing of "Experience."

> I am not satisfied to let it go with the aphorism that the style is the man. The man's ideas would then be some element of his style. So would his deeds. But I would narrow the definition. His deeds are his deeds; his ideas are his ideas. His style is the way he carries himself toward his ideas and deeds. Mind you if he is downspirited it will be all he can do to have the ideas without the carriage. The style is out of his superfluity. It is the mind skating circles round itself as it moves forward. Emerson had one of the noblest least egotistical of styles. By comparison with it Thoreau's was conceited, Whitman's bumptious.

In his use of the word "superfluity" to describe stylistic energies of mind and in his figuration of thinking as skating, Frost is conflating a passage I have already discussed in "Experience" with a second, where Emerson says that "we live amid surfaces and the true art of life is to skate well on them."

Just as thought in Emerson is put in opposition to thinking, so merely to "live amid surfaces" is here opposed to "the art of life." Action, or "skating," is a way of getting round intellectual concepts, which would be among the things he would call surfaces. Surfaces include ideas and texts. We live among these as among so many "circles" or discursive formations. "Art" itself—meaning the performative acts out of which texts are produced—allows us a stylish, studied, graceful, and cool way of moving around these surfaces, with an always forward-looking superfluity of motion. Style represents a movement of mind as against the stasis achieved by former movements that have become textualized or intellectualized.

The human mind gives evidence of itself therefore in two places at once. It is both in the skating, the transitional movement, and it is in or on the surfaces or texts around which the skating moves. There are repeated figurations of this kind in William James, who, with so many American writers from Emerson to Parkman to Stein, Hemingway, Mailer, and Joyce Carol Oates, likes to talk about workers or explorers or athletes or warriors when they have in mind their own activity of thinking/writing. In "What Pragmatism Means" James defines a pragmatist, for example, as one who "turns his back resolutely and once for all upon a lot of inveterate habits dear to professional philosophers. He turns away from abstraction and insufficiency, from verbal solutions, from bad *a priori* reasons, from fixed principles, closed systems, and pretended absolutes and origins. He turns towards concreteness and adequacy, towards facts, towards action, and towards power. . . . It means the open air and possibilities of nature, as against dogma, artificiality, and the pretence of finality in truth."

Rousing, get-up-and-go talk, from a man all the while

sitting at his desk, pen in hand. Philosophical and literary-critical proponents of "action" similarly begin and remain at the desk, writing about action even while writing is the essential form their action takes. James's "turning" can only mean verbal troping, and this can be said as well for the he-man strenuosities favored by other American writers, which include farming, bullfighting, woodcutting, boxing, or pathfinding. All of these are metaphors for that anti-intellectualism (not to be confused with being anti-intellectual) which over the last one hundred fifty years has united Emersonian writers to the pragmatism defined by James, both in his essays and in his correspondence. I am thinking at the moment of his correspondence with Henri Bergson, the philosopher known for his arguments on behalf of *élan vital* and in favor of evolution as determined less by natural selection than by creative desire. These influences are seldom recognized by their beneficiaries, and T. S. Eliot is no different in this from Wallace Stevens, when he transfers his never-admitted debts to Emerson and James to figures who to him seem less provincial, as in his early expressions of admiration for Bergson, whose lectures he heard in Paris in 1910–1911.[14]

To "turn away from insufficiency," to "skate" on or around "surfaces"—this is, then, a way of saying that you are in a slippery but by no means anxious relation to earlier creations, texts, or truths. It can also put you into an actively skeptical, antagonistic/flirtatious relation to your own writing, especially as you discover that it, too, might, as the words hit the pages, be gravitating dangerously toward "pretended absolutes." Thus Emerson will sometimes quite abruptly disclaim a phrase which is endorsed even by his own title, as we have seen him do in "Self-Reliance." The self for Emerson appears only *in* its own doings, *in* its workings, *in* its actions with words—*in* movements which turn back against any self, or on any assemblage of words as it may have been constituted even a moment ago. That immediately prior self becomes only one more object of scrutiny. Better, then, not to *assert* a self; do not "prate," only "speak" in some more pliant way, or say nothing. George Kateb has something of this sort in mind when he proposes that Whitman speaks in a manner designed to accept conventions without also conforming to them[15]; Whitman famously says of himself that he is "Both in and out of the game, and watching and wondering at it." Thoreau speaks similarly of "being beside ourselves in a sane way."

"Conscious of myself / And of some other being," to recall Wordsworth in the same mood, the Emersonian individual exists not in its assertions; it exists in a continuous struggle with the language by which it tries to get expressed. Except for section 4 of *Nature,* Emerson only very intermittently addresses himself to language as a problem. His concern for it is for the most part buried in metaphors having to do with repose and transition, action and antagonism, freedom and fate, and, in "Self-Reliance," with the degree to which speech "commits" or imprisons you. The inference to be drawn is that when you put yourself into words on any given occasion you are in fact not expressing yourself. In choosing to be understood, you are to some extent speaking in conformity to usages and in harmony with assumptions shared by your auditors. At best, then, you are expressing only some part of yourself. And since speaking or writing are by nature forms of emphasis, even that part or fragment of self so revealed probably misrepresents the full measure of your feeling. Emerson here again anticipates William James, who pragmatically distrusted language for the degree to which its structural principles support cultural absolutes. Because it tends to fix our attention on substantives at the expense of the transitive components in any sentence, syntax for James caters to an unfortunate human taste for fixities, for certainties, for the introspective habits that these encourage, and thus for inertia. It was James's desperate fear of all of these, along with his own hypochondria, which help explain his idealization of physical activity and such excesses of it in his own life as the mountain climbing episodes that ultimately brought on a nearly fatal heart attack.

The Emersonian individual, of which James's individual is a version, "turns" continually and quizzically on its own doubled and fractured self, aware that one part is apt to be saying more than some other part can accept. Either it is speaking with "éclat," as Emerson puts it in "Self-Reliance," out of the false confidence bred of current usage, or it is saying less than it feels like saying, because it lacks the superfluity promised by its own genius. The result is that we do not ever fully mean what we say or say what we mean. Reading Emerson is especially difficult, and exciting, because rhetorically he usually seems to be insisting that he *does* emphatically mean what he is saying. In fact, his rhetoric is at times symptomatic of his worry that if he does fail assertively to speak out he will, by being reticent, misrepresent the "flow of experience" within him, even more than he would by using excessive or falsifying words. He writes out of a fear that he might block and therefore forever lose some momentary, partial conviction simply because he desperately wants instead, and impossibly, to discover a formula that will express fully whatever is going on inside him. His words at such moments take on all the passionate and local force that any one of the different "lords of life" can give them. By the late essay "Fate" he has become quite explicit about the process:

> But if there be irresistible dictation, this dictation understands itself. If we must accept Fate, we are not less compelled to affirm liberty, the significance of the individual, the grandeur of duty, the power of character. This is true, and that other is true. But our geometry cannot span these extreme points, and reconcile them. What to do? By obeying each thought frankly, by harping, or, if you will, pounding on each string, we learn at last its power. By the same obedience to other thoughts, we learn theirs, and then comes some reasonable hope of harmonizing them.

Along the way, much has to be abandoned—sons and lovers, thoughts one had deemed precious, ideas of oneself more precious still. In "Experience," at once the most personal and most intricately shaped of his essays, he admits at the end that "I know better than to claim any completeness in my picture. I am a fragment, and this is a fragment of me."

The coda of the essay begins with a naming of the "lords of life"—Illusion, Temperament, Succession, Surface, Surprise, Reality, Subjectiveness—a listing somewhat different from the one given in the essay's introductory poem; it is to be inferred that each of these "lords" corresponds to a section of the essay. They are listed, he says, in no order of preference, but only "as I found them in my way." "In my way"—casually, according to my habit, as they happened to inspire me, and also, as I came to discover, only after the fact, how much each of these "lords" has limited or obstructed my access to unmediated reality. The remainder of the paragraph is one of the most affecting he ever wrote in its Shakespearean audacity and eloquence. I refer in particular to the Shakespeare who is the shaping presence in the final speeches of some of the tragedies. There we find the dying hero—Lear or Cleopatra or Othello, along with their attendants—slipping into tones and inflections that remind us, at what seem particularly unpropitious moments, of how still indestructibly alive in them are the failings and foibles which brought them to this pass, flaws which, recollected at a finale, might be expected to blur rather than enhance the grandeur of their parting. Inflections and tonalities of a similar kind can be heard as Emerson arrives at his own parting from this essay. It is as if, having gotten past each of the "lords of life" that were in his way, he is at last reduced to some bare rock of self. Bare not in the sense of totally naked, since there can be no such condition for anything constituted by language, but bare in the sense of exposed.

"Bareness," however, like any other of his favored terms, leads a complex life in Emerson's prose. It often describes cultural denudation in the New World, but he can view this denudation either as promising or dispiriting. For an example of the latter, there is a passage in the Journals of October 1851 where he admits to being "struck with a feeling of great poverty; my bareness! my bareness! seems America to say"; for an example of the former, of bareness as an inducement to sublimity, there is the bare common in *Nature*. "Bareness" can be similarly conceived in either mood in Ruskin, in Charles Peirce's idea of Firstness ("The idea of the present instant, which, whether it exists or not, is naturally thought as a point of time in which no thought can take place or any detail be separated, is an idea of Firstness"),[16] and in the Stevens of "The Snow Man."

And yet in "Experience" Emerson becomes especially eloquent about bareness and reduction, infusing them with a complication all his own. The complication derives from his conviction that we live inescapably amid surfaces, that we constitutionally mistake these for reality, and never more-so than when we perceive any one of them through any of our humors or our moods, including grief, or through the "prison of glass which we cannot see," which is temperament. "The individual is always mistaken," he repeats in consecutive sentences in "Experience." This wholly unexpected insistence, coming as it does from the champion of individualism, is to be understood, I think, only by something several paragraphs later, in a passage on "bareness" which I have previously read as an image mostly of cultural denudation. It is telling us, as I now see it, that any access to superfluity, to the power for new creation, depends on the admission that our own subjectivity, which we like to associate with depth, is itself bare and barren, itself the antagonist of superfluity: "We cannot say too little of our constitutional necessity of seeing things under private aspects, or saturated with our humors. And yet is the God the native of these bleak rocks. That need makes in morals the capital virtue of self-trust. We must hold hard to this poverty, however scandalous, and by more vigorous self-recoveries, after the sallies of action, possess our axis more firmly."

This is a passage full of perplexities. "Sallies of action" sounds derogatory, "sallies" implying a sudden or capricious departure from bounds or customs. "Sallies of action" may thereby resemble Thoreau's "extra-vagance," and yet it does so advisedly, in expectation of retreat to some more poised form of mobility that takes place on or at "our axis." What is this "axis"? In its elusiveness of location it resembles the self which, in "Self-Reliance," is described as "that which relies because it works and is." I take this axis to refer to a Jamesian turning place which steadies us as we make turns or tropes. It is to be located by each of us, presumably, at the divide of his or her nature. In "Fate," this divide is called "our polarity." "Man," he goes on to say, "*is* a stupendous antagonism, a dragging together of the poles of the Universe" (my emphasis). The word "sallies" cautions against our having too giddy a sense of the possibilities of "action" as it occurs under the aegis of Fate. The alleged Emersonian idealization of "action," a term whose elusiveness is discussed in the Introduction, is thus still more radically abridged in "Experience," no less than is his customary idealization of individuality. Just as he warns against a self-assertiveness in speech which can make you a "committed" or imprisoned person, so in the essay on Goethe he warns, with reference to actions publically undertaken, that "men's actions are too strong for them. Show me a man who has acted, and who has not been the victim and slave of his action." Emerson must have come very close to being crippled and silenced, as was William James even more nearly, by his suspicion that *all* assertions of the self in speech and action are destructive of individuality. Instead he chose to turn the suspicion into a modus operandi by which his essays find occasion to say anything that comes to mind so long as he can then find some way to unsay it. As a result, the full expression of one's limitations is transformed into an expression of one's freedom from limitation. By fully accepting limitations and fate you discover a possible way to elude them, for a time at least, if only by listening to and thereby doubling yourself.

One such limitation is subjectiveness or subjectivity, though it is often thought to be the area of inner freedom. In Emerson there is no such "inner" place to begin with. You are free only when you are getting out of whatever closet you are in, including your idea of yourself. The whole of the essay "Experience" is an effort to get away from or out of the subjectivity it generates, a subjectivity supposed by most readers to be the very source of the essay's and of our own imaginative richness and superfluity. Instead, he asks you to submit to the *poverty* of subjectivity, the poverty of self. At the same time however, he says, you must stubbornly hold onto it, even though it is "scandalous," even though, as a root meaning of "scandalous" suggests, it also causes you to stumble. Poverty is *all* you have to hold onto, and it is only *in* this poverty—born of the "rock"—that you find "the God." He does not say God but "the God," referring thereby to some generative, creative power that in fact only temporarily allows expression of itself through the medium of a human being. This is to be rephrased by Stevens in his great late poem "The Rock":

As if nothingness contained a métier,
A vital assumption, an impermanence
In its permanent cold, an illusion so desired
That the green leaves came and covered the high rock.

The voice of poverty sounds its patient (though in Emerson its sometimes slightly supercilious) awareness that it does not, and for good reason should not, grieve for anything—not for the loss of sons and lovers or its failed trust in the "lords of life" or in God or in its own inescapable subjectivity. While all these are inventions of the human mind, it has also been given to the mind to understand that it, too, is a gift to whoever and for whatever moment possesses some part of it. You deserve that gift only to the extent that you ignorantly (or knowingly) continue the work of nature, continue in James's words to "build it out." To recall "Pragmatism and Humanism": "We *add,* both to the subject and to the predicate part of reality. The world stands really malleable, waiting to receive its final touches at our hands. Like the kingdom of heaven, it suffers human violence willingly. Man *engenders* truths upon it."

No specific individual, no specific work of art needs to have existed, however, to insure this "engendering." Not Waldo, not Emerson, no one. The plays of Shakespeare do not need to have existed, or his works; however grateful we are for them, they are examples of superfluity. When, in an Emersonian mood in *The Geographical History of America,* Gertrude Stein says that if a masterpiece were lost nothing would in fact be lost because after all we did not have it, she means that any masterpiece is a gift in history from the human mind, which is timeless. And yet the mind which helped create the masterpiece is also enlarged by it. Even if the text disappears, the workings that produced it are forever after encoded in that mind and they will produce a different but equivalent or greater masterpiece, conditioned by the different occasion, place, and personality of the creator. What Stein here calls "mind," Emerson calls "intellect," and he distinguishes it from "intellect constructive," to which it is anterior. This distinction allows that while writers are necessarily obliged by the language they use to express the historical moment in which they find themselves, they can also use that language to free themselves from any absolute obligation. They can so far transfigure historical discourse that they end up speaking to a posterity in no way bound by that discourse.

II

THE TRANSFIGURATION OF WORK

Any study of the idea of work in the literature of nations would be a massive undertaking. And it would become especially difficult at the inevitable point—it seems inevitable to me—where it has to confront authorial claims that writing is itself demonstrably hard work, work with language that manages to encompass the vocabularies, and therefore some of the reality, of most other kinds of work. Emily Dickinson had some such idea in mind, I suspect, when she wrote:

> Essential Oils—are wrung—
> The Attar from the Rose
> Be not expressed by Suns—alone—
> It is the gift of Screws—

Readers of her own time would have recognized in these lines a reference to a housewives' chore by which dried flower petals, or potpourri, are pressed so as to extract a fragrant essence. Readers then, and especially now, might also agree that she is referring to the way words are "wrung" or turned by the work this particular woman does at home, which is to write poems like this one. I hear a word being "wrung," for instance, in the phrase "not expressed by Suns—alone—" wherein this rare daughter of the muse claims equality in poetic status with putative brothers. Indeed, in the second and final stanza of this poem, she expresses the hope that, by virtue of her poetry, when it is discovered, she will achieve immortality of sorts in a poetic line nearly exclusively male:

> The General Rose—decay—
> But this—in Lady's Drawer
> Make Summer—When the Lady lie
> In Ceaseless Rosemary—

Just as attar of roses in a lady's drawer keeps its perfume after the lady and any roses have died, so "this"—this poem, when found in this lady's drawer by some future reader—will have kept its fragrance, even though the poet herself has passed on. She will therefore be forever remembered, as she herself remembers Shakespeare here—"There's rosemary, that's for remembrance." All this is to say that poetry is necessarily hard work. It is a wringing, a screwing, a turning of words, and its full rewards are to be realized only in the future. Readers of the future will discover, as we do now, that the poet has managed to leave traces of herself inscribed forever in our shared language. Without intending to, Dickinson is in this instance writing as an Emersonian pragmatist.

This idea—of writing as work, and especially work whose rewards are both immeasurable and postponed—is my main concern in this chapter, where I will be discussing some writers more firmly placed than Dickinson in an Emersonian pragmatist dispensation.[1] The writers I have most particularly in mind, along with Emerson, are William James (and to some extent John Dewey) in tandem with American poets of a discernibly similar temperament, like Thoreau, Whitman, Frost, Stein, and Stevens. These writers move us very quickly into troubled waters, and for several reasons. First of all, in the philosophical writings, no less than the poetry—I have been reading one no differently from the other—the correspondence between physical work and mental work, between manual labor and writing (which is no less an operation of the hands), is expressed with an eagerness that effectively blurs the social and cultural distinctions known to exist between these different kinds of activity. Second, the propositions about work done with pen and paper—that it is work done in earnest, that it is hard going, that it is just as purposeful, just as unsure of a profitable outcome as is work done in a field or a household—lead inevitably to a complication by which writing is described in metaphors of economic enterprise. A notorious example is William James's phrase in *Pragmatism:* "the practical cash-value." He applies this phrase to his own and to our work with words, and means to propose that the work represents an investment in the future of linguistic commodities. And third, this correspondence between day labor and desk labor is couched in terms meant to carry the aura of pastoral even while it is also meant to dispel its social hierarchies, wherein, as William Empson would have it, higher condescends to lower. The mode of address in my American examples is ostentatiously democratic; it aspires, as poetry in the pastoral traditions does not, to a general popular audience.

Indeed, to the very degree that Emersonian pragmatists insist that writing is a form of work there seems to be an implicit acknowledgment that, if writing were to be otherwise perceived, it might alienate the writers themselves from the larger human community they hope to please and persuade. This possibility is all the more troublesome when, as in the United States, the members of that community have themselves become determined, almost deadeningly so according to Tocqueville, upon social equality, or where, as in England in the seventeenth century, revolution has for a moment at least incited some degree of impatience with inherited status. Marvell's "Upon Appleton House," a Horatian meditation of nearly eight hundred lines on the social and cultural consequences of the English Civil War, offers stunning testimony to this. There is a moment in the poem, which I identified some years ago in *The Performing Self* as giving evidence of cultural crises, that has, so far as I make out, no precedent before Marvell in English poetry: a character is allowed at about the middle of the poem to step out of its fictional frame so as to comment on the literary manners of the author, to question the authority by which he has identified the workers in the poem by the use of literary and Biblical allusions.[2] Two stanzas previously, Marvell had said of the "tawny mowers" that they

> . . . seem like Israelites to be
> Walking on foot through a green sea.
> To them the grassy deeps divide,
> And crowd a lane to either side.

In the next stanzas it is revealed that one of the mowers has accidentally killed a small bird with his scythe and that it has been immediately grasped by a figure identified as "bloody Thestylis," a camp follower who brings food to the mowers:

> But bloody Thestylis, that waits
> To bring the mowing camp their cates,
> Greedy as kites has trussed it up,
> And forthwith means on it to sup;

> When on another quick she lights,
> And cries "He called us Israelites;
> But now, to make his saying true,
> Rails rain for quails, for manna dew."

Marvell is solicitous of the birds who, deprived of flight, have become in their lowness the victims of the mower's scythe. Obviously, he is analogously solicitous of himself. His poetic flight is just as rudely leveled and brought down, and so are his efforts to be condescending to his subjects through pastoral allusion:

> Unhappy birds! what does it boot
> To build below the grasses' root,
> When lowness is unsafe as height,
> And chance o'ertakes what scapeth spite.

Marvell, with some considerable misgivings, is staging a mini-revolution, one that marks the end of a culture that heretofore was happy to tolerate the kind of pastoral poetry he had chosen to write. By contrast, American writers, in their own post-revolutionary period, found no reason to invite the sort of social reprimand that Marvell visits on himself. They were instead convinced that once writers had earned recognition as workers of a sort they need never feel estranged from other kinds of workers who were building the new world. Compared to Marvell's witty, aristocratic, learned pastoralism, theirs is democratic, often humorous, and conversational. Under scrutiny, however, these Americans prove to be no less literary in their syntax, no less allusive (though surreptitiously so) in their idiom, than is Marvell. And by effectively disguising, often from themselves, their ultimate will to cultural supremacy, they become even harder to figure out than he is. I will be showing in detail the great subtlety by which, even as they reverse the position in which Marvell finds himself inconvenienced, they manage at the same time to reinstate the authority of literature.

They are able to do this effectively by seeming not to be doing it at all. One crucial step in the process involves the elevation of a hard day's work to the aesthetic status of literary work. There is nothing cynical in this operation; it is fully consistent with the most sincerely held Emersonian pragmatist convictions about work, and equally consistent with its idealizations of the profit motive. By a stunningly ideological maneuver, they manage to persuade themselves, and any reasonably sympathetic readers, that ordinary labor might, on occasion, offer some of the exaltations that can be derived from intellectual-literary pursuits. Having made such an allowance, they are then in a position to reverse the field. They can propose that the writing and reading of literature are, for America, an absolutely exemplary form of work.

Thus, for example, if the profits that come from field work are to be measured not only in dollars and cents but also in heightenings of consciousness that are immeasurable, so too, and even more evidently, are the profits of literary work. Literary work is socially repositioned, but only that it may regain its traditionally exalted status. It is no longer a monument to the past, and it does not offer the clarifications of life that might make us culturally dependent on certain texts. Rather it becomes a source of gratification that is full of vague promises as to the future. In that sense the gratifications that come from writing and reading resemble those which can result from the intense physical expenditures involved in common pursuits like field work, sexual intercourse, athletics, or exploration. In promoting this equation, Emersonian pragmatists intend to prove that writers of literature contribute no less than do day laborers, housewives, or adventurers to the dream which is America, a dream whose realization is forever being postponed.

Just as for Frost's apple picker there comes, as a release from work, some pleasurably drowsy, strangely expectant uncertainty, along with a blurred sense of the objects on which so much energy has been expended, so too there comes as a reward to Emersonian pragmatist readers and writers an equivalent feeling generated by literary language. Each of the writers I have mentioned uses a different word or formula to commend this condition of induced drift and disorientation. For Emerson the word is "abandonment," the giving up of positions already taken; for Thoreau it is "extravagance" or wandering off; for Whitman it is his reiterated "negligence" and images of lolling about; for James it is "vagueness" or "fringe"; for Stein it is an effect of what she calls "repetition"; for Stevens a reiterated "as if"; for Frost in evocations of sleepiness or the dream state, as in the poem "Mowing."

From the first two lines the speaker of that poem is, like Thoreau at Walden, indistinguishable from a worker in the field. This identification of poet with worker is nowhere encouraged in Marvell's mower poems, which inevitably come to mind, and while Marvell continuously alerts us to his poetic allusiveness, as if classical learning were a pleasure his readers are expected to share with him, Frost does his best to hide his allusiveness altogether, as if in deference to readers who are closer to field workers than to poetic ones. There is, however, another, profounder significance to Frost's deference. He is in effect saying that the allusiveness really is not his to claim anyway; it belongs to idioms anyone may pick up. The implication is that allusiveness is already present, and always has been, in the ordinary things we evoke.

Common to the Emersonian pragmatists is this acceptance of the fact that literary references are inherent in and ineradicable from daily speech. But even while these writers may therefore seem to be exalting quotidian work, they are, once again, doing nearly the opposite. They are trying to endow poetry, and poetic work on language, with a truly extraordinary degree of cultural and historical importance, as if it represents in itself the ideal achievement and attainment of *all* work. Poetry does not represent life; life, they suggest, represents poetry. This gives to poetry an importance which may legitimately seem both mad and maddening. More about that later, but first the poem:

There was never a sound beside the wood but one,
And that was my long scythe whispering to the ground.
What was it it whispered? I knew not well myself;
Perhaps it was something about the heat of the sun,
Something, perhaps, about the lack of sound—
And that was why it whispered and did not speak.
It was no dream of the gift of idle hours,
Or easy gold at the hand of fay or elf:
Anything more than the truth would have seemed too weak
To the earnest love that laid the swale in rows,

Not without feeble-pointed spikes of flowers
(Pale orchises), and scared a bright green snake.
The fact is the sweetest dream that labor knows.
My long scythe whispered and left the hay to make.

The comforting notion communicated here is that the voice belongs to a mower who just happens to be speaking to us in verse, and that we can relax into his words without worrying about his pulling a fast one. This notion is sustained in a number of ways. There is, for example, the specificity of physical details, like "the heat of the sun" or "the swale in rows" or "the pale orchises" or the "bright green snake," the last an image taken from Coleridge's "Christabel" and domesticated by the vivid, childlike word "scared." A poet might say "scared," but a laborer is far more likely to, especially since this particular would-be laborer is everywhere anxious to divest himself of evident knowingness about his own activity, and in phrases audibly colloquial: "I knew not well myself" or "perhaps it was something," and "something, perhaps." Does he know what he is saying when, in the first line, he puts the "woods" in conjunction with "sound?" Does he know that this is allusive to a Latin proverb—it makes its way into English as "the walls have ears"—to the effect that "fields have sight and woods have ears"? Similarly, "a snake in the grass" is a phrase so familiar that its classical origin, in Virgil's *Third Eclogue*, where "a snake lurks in the grass," is all but lost even to readers well versed in poetry, and surely to him. It is pure Emersonian genius to let the poet-as-common-laborer thus use common idioms that he does not know are also classical allusions, to let him show how tradition is most alive in us when we are least in a position to feel grateful for it.

Perhaps, too, the scythe "whispers" about the "heat of the sun" because this mower-poet himself dares only to whisper about his own close literary associations, presumptuous as these would sound to New Hampshire neighbors from someone whose first book, published when its author was nearly forty, is still a decade hence. He is claiming kinship, if they but knew, with Sidney and Shakespeare. One of his whispered allusions is to Shakespeare's song in *Cymbeline,* "Fear no more the heat o' th' sun," a song full of references, by the way, to doing your "worldly tasks" before you inevitably discover for yourself that "Golden lads and girls all must, / As chimney-sweepers, come to dust." And there is yet another "whispered" allusion in the same phrase, "the heat of the sun," an allusion to the first sonnet of *Astrophel and Stella,* where Sidney complains of having a "sun-burn'd brain." He means a brain oversaturated by his reading of his forebears.

Frost is equally wary of forebears. The first two lines—"There was never a sound beside the wood but one, / And that was my long scythe whispering to the ground"—I take as a hesitant assertion of originality from a poet who will later lay claim to it on the basis of a theory of what he calls in several of his letters "the sound of sense" or "sentence sounds."[3] In "never a sound but one" he is intimating that the sound of his poetry is and will be unique in this—or any—place. Nonetheless, I still whisper rather than speak aloud, he might as well be saying, because I am dazzled by the heat of the sun, those luminous predecessors. I must work especially hard not to become a poet derivative of the classics or of *The Golden Treasury*. Palgrave's famous collection of English poets, a book which Frost treasured, is further in evidence here, I think, in the claim that the whispers he does hear from his own scythe are "no dream of the gift of idle hours, / Or easy gold at the hand of fay or elf." His sounds are the result instead of the hard work required of anyone who will be at once indebted and original, dependent on linguistic inheritances and capable of troping them.

The more ambitious of the meanings I have tried to tease from this poem, the kind we all like to mistake for ultimate ones, are delicately recessed not within patent difficulties and allusions, as is often the case with poets in the line of Eliot, Pound, and Lowell, but within patent simplicities of diction and within a waywardness of phrasing that is shy about, yet fully possessed of, its own allusive possibilities. Like other work poems by Frost—including most obviously "After Apple-Picking," "Putting in the Seed," "Mending Wall," "The Tuft of Flowers," "The Ax-Helve," "Two Tramps in Mud Time" and "The Wood-Pile"— "Mowing," which is the earliest of these, manages to make the forms and processes of actual work into a version of literary archeology. The implication in all of them is that careful and intense ordinary labor, when applied to the things of this world, can gradually dissolve their commodity values into mythological ones. And this is just what any intense literary labor does, so it is suggested, when it digs into and transfigures words.

Frost's worker thereby *becomes* a poet by virtue of his labor, as Emerson everywhere promises he might. By intense application to a thing like hay, by "the divinity of muscular labor," as James calls it in "What Makes a Life Significant," the worker discovers what poets have always discovered by their intense application to a thing like language: namely, as Emerson says in "The Poet," that "language is the archives of history." The value of either of these things—of an object or of a word—is compounded by investments already made in them by our ancestors. They therefore invite comparable investments from us. Kenneth Burke nowhere more fully reveals his own Emersonian pragmatism than in an essay in *Language as Symbolic Action* called "What Are the Signs of What: A Theory of Entitlement." Thoreau frequently touches on this interplay of investment and entitlement, especially in the chapter of *Walden* called "The Bean Field." On that occasion, Thoreau, like Frost, is both a poet and an actual worker. He can claim that "it was no longer beans that I hoed, nor I that hoed beans," listing meanwhile his "outgoes" and income, along with measured quantities of harvest. He is one of those who, he says, "work in fields for the sake of tropes and expression," and yet, just as clearly, he is simultaneously a harvester of beans. "The result of my experience in raising beans," he concludes, is "a pecuniary profit . . . of 8.71\frac{1}{2}$."

These are only initial examples of an Emersonian pragmatist preoccupation with the profit of intense physical or mental work, work carried out, it should be clear, with a certain regard for form, rigor, and discipline. As a result of such work, it is suggested, you can escape from arbitrary divisions between past and present, while coming to a realization that physical objects which before seemed obdurate, or texts that seemed definitive, are in fact transitional, fluid, and indiscrete. As Emerson puts it in the shorter essay called "Nature": "But if, instead of identifying ourselves with the work"—by which he here means any product created by work—"we feel that the soul of the workman streams through us, we shall find the peace of the morning dwelling first in our hearts, and the fathomless powers of gravity and chemistry, and, over them, of life, preëxisting within us in their highest form."

While such Emersonian rhetoric scarcely helps clarify my argument at this juncture, it cannot be ignored on that account. It sounds opaquely grandiose, an instance of what exasperated even so devoted a friend as Henry James, Sr.: "Oh you man without a handle," he complained in 1843.[4] Henry's son William later made essentially the same claims for work as Emerson does, though in simpler terms—not that this spared him the complaint, from his friend Ralph Barton Perry, that he had "a pathological repugnance to the process of exact thought."[5] There is probably no way these writers can please practical or academically minded people, but then there is no connection whatever between being practical and being pragmatist. Work for "pecuniary profit" and work for "the sake of tropes," outdoor work and indoor work, bodily work with objects and mental work with words—the Emersonian pragmatist attempt to fuse and confuse these finds its most notorious expression, as already suggested, in James's phrase the "practical cash-value."

In the passage where James actually uses that phrase, which occurs in the chapter of *Pragmatism* called "What Pragmatism Means," it is applied quite narrowly to words, and so can have nothing whatever to do with short-term gains. James is instead attacking our tendency to sell ourselves short, to circumscribe ourselves by a dependence on abstractions. We seek dependence, he says, "in the shape of some illuminating or power-bringing word or name," or in explanations on which we can "rest" and that make further work unnecessary. "But if you follow the pragmatic method," he continues, "you cannot look on any such word as closing your quest. You must bring out of each word its practical cash-value, set it at work within the stream of your experience. It appears less as a solution, then, than as a program for more work, and more particularly as an indication of the ways in which existing realities may be *changed*."

Using the idea of work as a focus, I am attempting to locate in Emerson, James, and their associates an aesthetic having to do with the uses of language, and especially with language in its relation to the past. It needs to be kept in mind all the while, however, that the philosophers Emerson and James write less like philosophers or theorists than like their own poetic inheritors. They are like poets in their frequent resort to dizzying metaphors, in an allusiveness and elusiveness of phrasing that is to become a feature of the poetry of Frost, Eliot, and Stevens, and in their challenges to that authority over meaning said to be exercised by the customary structure of sentences and paragraphs. They never bother, however, fully to puzzle out the literary, much less the social consequences of their inferable linguistic theories. It is left to Gertrude Stein to take her teacher James at his word—"William James taught me all I know," she is reported to have said to Richard Wright[6] —and then to do him one better by demonstrating with the brilliant intransigence of *Tender Buttons* or "Stanzas in Meditation" how strange prose and poetry would indeed become should such challenges to linguistic authority as his find their way into actual practice.

Thus, while a philosophy of language can be inferred or pieced together from the writings of Emerson and James, there are in fact only a very few calculated discussions about language to be found in their works. And when these do occur, they very often disappear, as does philosophical rigor, into metaphors like "cash-value" or "streams," or into such figures as Emerson uses in "The Poet" when he says that "all language is vehicular and transitive, and is good, as ferries and horses are, for conveyance, not as farms and houses are, for homestead." The effect of such metaphors is to press still further the implication allowed in other ways—that work with language can somehow occur anywhere at all and can therefore have measurable effects outside poetry, upon the economic, social, or historical order of things. Thus, when James directly addresses "you" in the passage from *Pragmatism,* and tells you that you must look for "an indication of the ways in which existing realities may be *changed,*" he is trying to persuade you, and himself, to forget that even according to the passage itself this "indication" can become available only in the difficult and prolonged work he has described with "each word," the kind of work customarily entrusted only to a poet or philosopher. "You" must "bring out . . . its practical cash-value" and you "must set it at work" within some sort of stream.

It is necessary to wonder just where *in* the world this "bringing out" and this "setting to work" can occur. Does it occur in the joking, punning, and verbal play of lettuce pickers? In reflections on language while you are doing the laundry? In linguistic analyses carried on among carpenters? There is really only one place where the activity described by James or Emerson is ever carried out concertedly and effectively, and that is in writing and reading, especially of literature. And it is with the hope of getting round this limitation and ameliorating its socially alienating effects that Emerson, James, and their poetic successors set out to disguise their own extraordinary degree of literariness, while discouraging, by the very semblance of aphoristic availability, any attempt to reduce their sentences to intellectualist formulas.

Their efforts to seem culturally available make them, in my view, more and not less difficult. Emerson was an immensely popular lecturer while being famous for opacity. Nearly all of James's writing, after *Principles of Psychology*, began as public lectures. Frost sought a wide audience, increasingly to his own disadvantage as a great poet; and when she wrote for *The Saturday Evening Post* Gertrude Stein was only confirming her assumption that she wrote for everybody. There is at the very heart of the Emersonian pragmatist enterprise with language, and in its concept of work, a compulsion to evade the fact (as I take it to be) that the work with language which they recommend and exemplify is so special a discipline that it can legitimately hope, despite James's gusto, to have only an indirect and minimal effect on existing realities, and can probably have little effect at all on the nature of work done beyond the study or on the page. Emersonian pragmatism, as represented by them, can claim social or communal efficacy only by to some extent cheating on itself. I agree with George Kateb when he suggests that Dewey is one of those Emersonians who sometimes falsify Emerson. Commenting on a liberal tendency especially threatening to Emersonian individualism—the tendency to guide or administer or engineer "greater togetherness, greater discipline, and greater group identity"—Kateb remarks on the docility thereby produced, and identifies Dewey, with T. H. Green, as among those "social liberals" who "urge so much mutuality that they betray the very idea of [individual] rights. They make rights merely instrumental to a society-wide and abstract mutuality."[7]

"Literature," says Emerson in "Circles," "is a point outside of our hodiernal circle, through which a new one may be described." To whom does "our" refer here? At any one time in the world there are alive only a very few who write what can be called literature. Most of the world's population cannot even read, and the number of persons capable of the sort of reading called for in these chapters is infinitesimal. Emerson and James are quite properly shy, though James tends to hide his shyness in bluster, about directly advancing the notion that the work of writing literature and of reading it can in itself do more than provide exemplary metaphors for action in the world. And to our great, if as yet unrealized, benefit, they and their poetic successors cast out altogether the fraudulent notion that literature is a monument to redemptive values and that it can help save us from the ravages of history. For them literature is a metaphor for work with language, work which just might possibly *begin* to help change existing realities, and only then if the work is carried on endlessly.[8]

There is absolutely nothing, no texts, to lean back on. Ideally, one is persuaded instead to join us in those "symbolic actions" adduced from literary texts by that remarkable Emersonian pragmatist reader, Kenneth Burke.[9]

It is well to remember, on that score, that there are in fact very few characters in literature who are represented as actually at work on anything other than language. We are told that they are gainfully employed, sometimes, but all we hear or see them doing to and for one another is using words. Hawthorne's *The Blithedale Romance* is to some extent a comic representation of this disparity. Almost without exception Henry James's characters are rich enough to be unemployed, in order that they may give full time to exhibitions of fine consciousness. And yet James is forever talking about his own religion of doing—"It all takes doing—and I do," he writes in a letter to Henry Adams in 1914. His prefaces are largely about how *he* works and composes, using his layabout characters as "compositional resources." This is to some degree true of all writers, even when, as in Dreiser or Zola, their characters are wage earners.

Imagined by its authors as essentially an enactment of work with words, literature is then allowed to register its superiority over all other kinds of work in the management and transformation of "hard facts," to recall the title of a relevant book by Philip Fisher. A work of literature always involves an effort in language to transcend the work's own thematic materials, whether these have to do with imperial power, colonialism, sexual courting, or the other arts. It is the place where metaphors for other kinds of work are brought into competitive play with the compositional designs of literary work itself. Thus, in the essay "Experience," Emerson admits that the language for the representation of gains and losses, even of his own progeny, partakes necessarily of the restrictive language of finance and economy. To assume from this that his own views of loss and gain, or that his view of life and creativity, are bound in by the market economy is to fail as a reader. It is to miss entirely the effort by which he successfully puts economic terminologies "at work within the stream of [his own] experience." Emerson's resort to market metaphors is scarcely meant to suggest that we are merely the pawns of overdetermined vocabularies. His task rather is to demonstrate how, to some extent, he—and therefore we—can work with and beyond them. "The prison-house of language" is the soap opera of theory. Human beings do indeed continually discover their fate in language—not surprisingly, since it is there, after all, that they seek definitions for themselves. Just as continually, however, they discover that language can be the means by which they can get off the hook. There are many places other than literature where such work with language goes on, and yet literature remains one of the indispensable places, the more so since it is there that linguistic action is designed also to give pleasure.

In order to take advantage of this, readers must learn to do for themselves some version of the work being done word by word *in* the writing, work that continually exceeds and changes what any text seems for awhile to have settled on. The legitimation of criticism, according to Emerson in "The Poet," is "in the mind's faith, that the poems are a corrupt version of some text in nature, with which they ought to be made to tally." As we have seen, this statement gives an Emersonian twist to distinctions made in our own day between texts and works by a textual theorist like G. Thomas Tanselle. And it prepares us to be told a bit later on in "The Poet" that "An imaginative book renders us much more service at first, *by stimulating us through its tropes,* than afterward, when we arrive at the precise sense of the author" (my emphasis). Of course we never do arrive at any such "precise sense." Indeed his point is that the value of a book is to be found in its movements, its verbal actions, its twists and turns of words.

To read in accordance with these verbal actions is to be truly and most rigorously historical, for the reason that such acts require us as readers—and here I am quoting Dewey's *Art as Experience*—to "include relations comparable to those which the original producer underwent." Coming as close as possible, *while* we read, to duplicating the actions which went into the writing—actions inevitably of cultural resistance as well as of conformity—readers will discover, as Thoreau, in anticipation of Dewey, puts it in his Journal for January 7, 1844, that "Writing may be either the record of a deed or a deed. It is nobler when it is a deed." Or, to return to Emerson's "Art," we look to writing not for meanings but for "signs of power," "tokens of the everlasting effort to produce."

Those values which, we are assured, reside in the past and especially in its literature—what more can be said of them, indeed, but that they are "signs of power"? How, except as signs, do we get to know them? Of what use are these signs once we have them? To Emersonian pragmatists, questions of this sort are unavoidable, and the answers they proffer to them substantially disprove the frequent allegation that Emersonians are busy, in A. Bartlett Giamatti's phrase, "jettisoning history." In the writings of Emerson and his successors, the past is the very site of work because for them language is itself the site of work; this past, or its instrumentality in language, is the place where, if anywhere, new truth is, as James says, "funded": "I have already insisted," he writes in "Pragmatism's Conception of Truth," "on the fact that truth is made largely out of previous truths." Whatever seems to us new, as he can be recalled saying in "Pragmatism and Humanism," whatever comes to us "without the human touch . . . has immediately to become humanized in the sense of being squared, assimilated, or in some way adapted, to the humanized mass already there."

For Emerson, Thoreau, and James, for Frost, Stevens, and Stein, each very different in manner from the other, the past is best understood and made useful to the present when a way is found by which the creative efforts inferable from the productions of the past are, by a hermeneutical leap of faith, replicated and changed within the different linguistic and historical conditions of the present. This leap of faith may be prompted by an irreverence toward the past as past, the past as a series of monuments, but it requires an identification nonetheless with those in the past whose energies brought those monuments into existence. It requires a determination to do the work by which those energies can be reconstituted and redirected.

To the extent—and it is only to an extent—that some such view of the cultural past is expressed in T. S. Eliot's "Tradition and the Individual Talent," the essay owes more to Emerson and William James than, say, to Clive Bell or

Dora Marsden.[10] Eliot's declarations of faith in what he calls "the mind of Europe" are more Emersonian than he wanted to acknowledge, since far from denying that America first existed in that mind—included, as it is, in Emerson's "old paternal mind"—any true Emersonian pragmatist allows even for the possibility that the idea of America may come to its best fruition not on the American landmass at all, but on the Eurasian. Whitman concedes no less about America's European past, especially early on, as when, in the opening of the preface to the 1855 edition of *Leaves of Grass,* he says that "America does not repel the past or what it has produced under its forms." America perceives the past as a "corpse . . . slowly borne from the eating and sleeping rooms of the house," where life in the present is being carried on. But it also "perceives" that "its action" (action, that is, initiated by what is now a corpse) "has descended to the stalwart and wellshaped heir who approaches." I take this corpse to be a version of what Dewey will later call the "products" of the past. We have heard him say in *Democracy and Education,* for example, that "the study of past *products,*" a word which he underlines, "will not help us understand the present, because the present is not due to the products." It is due, he continues in true Emersonian fashion, "to the life of which they were the products." For the word "life" he could as easily have substituted the word "work." "The solar chariot is junk," according to Stevens's *Notes Toward a Supreme Fiction,* even while in the same poem he extols the *idea* of the sun which helped produce the now derelict image.

There may be occasional murmurs in these writers of an anxiety of influence, that immensely useful phrase by which

Harold Bloom so deftly transported Emerson into contemporary theory, but it does not seem to figure importantly in their theory of production.[11] Rather, they exude a quiet confidence that the texts of the past are less essential than the inferable work which produced them. It is doubtful that Stevens is revealing an anxiety of influence simply because he fails to confess his traceable indebtedness to Emerson, anymore than is Eliot in failing similarly to acknowledge Whitman. Like nearly all other American writers of the nineteenth as well as the twentieth century, they perhaps wanted only to avoid the appearance of provinciality by associating themselves with European rather than with native figures. Emerson himself did no less. This tendency in American intellectual careers is evident enough even in our own period, especially among professionalist academic critics who remain, for instance, stubbornly indifferent to the possibility that James and Dewey "were not only waiting at the end of the dialectical road which analytic philosophy traveled," but, as Richard Rorty goes on to say in *Consequences of Pragmatism,* "are waiting at the end of the road which, for example, Foucault and Deleuze are currently traveling."

Later American writers (and critics) fail to announce their indebtedness to earlier ones for a reason more important, however, than the fear of appearing merely insular and unfashionable. In the passages I have been citing, the combination of funereal gratitude with liberation reveals, I think, an Emersonian conviction that in fact no great writers now or then, here or there, ever wholly own or pretend to own what they produce; it is corporately owned by all of them and issues from a "genius" to which no individual can claim exclusive rights. Originality is something in which all of us own a share.

The relation of a present to a past writer can be like the relation Whitman proposes for himself with the animals of the field:

> They bring me tokens of myself. . . . they evince them
>   plainly in their possession.
> I do not know where they got these tokens,
> I must have passed that way untold times ago and
>   negligently dropped them,
> Myself moving forward then and now and forever.
>
> ("Song of Myself")

Finding expression here and frequently in Emerson, as in the shorter essay called "Nature," is, in Burke's phrase, a theory of entitlement, a phrase that is the subtitle to his essay "What Are the Signs of What." Put simply, a theory of entitlements, while allowing for the common assumption that words are the signs of things, proposes that the reverse of this may also be true: that things are the signs of words. That is, the things we look at already carry with them a fund of association which empowers, even prompts the words by which they can then be represented. Things are "funded" by the previous human uses which have been made of them. Is the word "rose" a sign of a flower? Yes, but it is a flower that has by now itself become a sign of, say, love or perfection or mortality or beauty, so much so that Stein decided at one point that we have had enough of such roses: "rose is a rose is a rose is a rose." She has no illusions that by such iteration she can actually make this be the case with roses; she is saying, rather, that the human mind, which has already made so much of roses, can also, as that mind now works in her, decreate and then recreate the word. And even as Stein is extending James's idea of "previous truths," she is looking past him to Emerson, in whose "Self-Reliance" (as I noted nearly thirty years ago in *A World Elsewhere*), there is a passage on roses of which her own is a revision.

According to this theory of entitlements, our language is full of essentially poetic associations, and anyone who uses it is therefore to some degree a poet. So that when I speak of "poetry and pragmatism" I again mean not simply that some pragmatist philosophers have had an influence on poets; I mean that in their own uses of words they too are poets, just as the poets are also philosophers. In his 1889 essay "Philosophical Conceptions and Practical Results," James says that "philosophers are after all like poets," because "They are, if I may use a simile, so many spots, or blazes,—blazes made by the axe of the human intellect on the trees of the otherwise trackless forest of human experience." And though he says that we of a later time therefore "bless their names," no names are mentioned, and in an echo of Whitman's admission that the tokens he discovers were "negligently dropped," he says of his poets and philosophers that the character of their operation is "thin and spotty and half-casual." I take this to mean that great spirits do not become finicky about authorial claims to specific creations; they care about work and about the signs of work. These signs are forever mixed into the wilderness of only possible meaningfulness; no final or possessive claim can be made of them, for them, or with them. Frost and Stevens are enchanted with this idea of signs, notably in

Frost's great sonnet "Never Again Would Birds' Song Be the Same" and in one of Stevens's finest shorter poems, "A Postcard from the Volcano."[12]

By locating among works by different authors so many repetitions—of images, phrases, ideas, mannerisms—I want to suggest that, far from exhibiting anxiety or even any consciousness of borrowing, these writers simply feel *entitled* to such repetitions, supposing as they do that not only in literature but in the things of this world are to be found centuries-old traces of sometimes anonymous human work. Stevens, in the poem just mentioned, puts it beautifully when he says,

> Children picking up our bones
> . . . least will guess that with our bones
> We left much more, left what still is
> The look of things, left what we felt
> At what we saw.

While working within a theory of entitlements and cultural transmissions, Emersonian pragmatist writers are also fully conscious of the fact, as Eric Hobsbawm would have it, that tradition is not merely something in the air.[13] It is evidenced, rather, by a *continuing* work of invention. But the special and quite wonderful suggestion in many of the passages I have cited is that, as Eliot insisted, any possession of tradition and of its treasures cannot be a willed or even a fully conscious one. It comes to you, as in Frost's "After Apple-Picking," by some equivalent of that dream state which can be the eventual reward of the exhaustions of labor. Releasing yourself to the intensities of the discipline of work, you discover that the marks left by poets and philosophers are, as James says, "half casual," more than can be willed into existence by any single individual effort.

T. S. Eliot calls for a place in this particular cluster of writers which has never adequately been given him, except for some mostly general remarks about the evidences of Whitman in his poetry. He has been relegated, as indeed he asked to be, to certain modernist and European developments which, while chronologically following the inceptions of the American ones I have been sketching, can now be recognized—especially when it comes to the function of language as part of any search for truths—as being relatively less sophisticated. On that score, Emersonian pragmatism has more affinities with post-structuralist than with modernist theory. My own reading of Eliot, beginning with an appreciation in *The Performing Self* of how he confutes the meanings usually ascribed to him, becomes adversely critical only when it confronts an Eliot who chose in his essays to advance himself as cultural prophet. He often allowed his powerfully affecting and disruptive vagueness, in his prose as well as in his poetry, to be dissipated by the large cultural pretentions of the wasteland ethos and by his participations in the gloomy Christianizing pedagogies of some of his New Critical admirers. That vagueness in Eliot's early poetry owes as much to Whitman and James as to the always mentioned Laforgue, while his deservedly most renowned essay, "Tradition and the Individual Talent," can be read, at many of its most crucial points, as a reflection of Emerson—as when, to add to evidence already given, he argues that the poet "must be quite aware of the obvious fact that art never improves, but that the material of art is never quite the same," or that "the difference between the present and the past is that the conscious present is an awareness of the past in a way and to an extent which the past's awareness of itself cannot show." There are perceptible echoes here of the essays "Art" and "Intellect," and more complex echoes of the great essay "History," where recovery of the past, along with a concomitant dissolution of facticity and of the private self, is directly attributed to intensive "work," much as it is in Eliot's famous dictum that tradition "cannot be inherited, and if you want it you must obtain it by great labour."

I want to turn now to three paragraphs in "History." They occur just after Emerson's challenge to what he calls "the solid angularity of facts" and after his admiring mention of Napoleon for asking " 'What is History . . . but a fable agreed upon?' " The writing at this point is dense even for him, exhibiting his characteristic refusal to clarify his own confusing uses of the same or related words. He does not sort out the confusions because they represent for him the reality within which we must try to move, using language as our instrument while knowing that it might also be temporarily immobilizing.

I will be looking in detail at two or three examples of how Emerson generates his necessary and salutary confusions, but I first want to quote the whole passage because it so masterfully registers most of the complexities that bind the idea of work for these writers to the idea of cultural recovery and renewal:

> We are always coming up with the emphatic facts of history in our private experience, and verifying them here. All history becomes subjective; in other words,

there is properly no history; only biography. Every mind must know the whole lesson for itself,—must go over the whole ground. What it does not see, what it does not live, it will not know. What the former age has epitomized into a formula or rule for manipular convenience, it will lose all the good of verifying for itself, by means of the wall of that rule. Somewhere, sometime, it will demand and find compensation for that loss by doing the work itself. Ferguson discovered many things in astronomy which had long been known. The better for him.

History must be this or it is nothing. Every law which the state enacts indicates a fact in human nature; that is all. We must in ourselves see the necessary reason of every fact,—see how it could and must be. So stand before every public and private work; before an oration of Burke, before a victory of Napoleon, before a martyrdom of Sir Thomas More, of Sidney, of Marmaduke Robinson; before a French Reign of Terror, and a Salem hanging of witches, before a fanatic Revival, and the Animal Magnetism in Paris, or in Providence. We assume that we under like influence should be alike affected, and should achieve the like; and we aim to master intellectually the steps and reach the same height or the same degradation, that our fellow, our proxy, has done.

All inquiry into antiquity,—all curiosity respecting the Pyramids, the excavated cities, Stonehenge, the Ohio Circles, Mexico, Memphis,—is the desire to do away this wild, savage, and preposterous There or Then, and introduce in its place the Here and the Now. Belzoni digs and measures in the mummy-pits and pyramids of Thebes, until he can see the end of the difference between the monstrous work and himself. When he has satisfied himself, in general and in detail, that it was made by such a person as he, so armed and so motived, and to ends to which he himself should also have worked, the problem is solved; his thought lives along the whole line of temples and sphinxes and catacombs, passes through them all with satisfaction, and they live again to the mind, or are *now*.

A fusion of opacity with familiarity of phrasing is an accomplishment of style cherished by Emerson no less than by Frost, and a good example is the best-known sentence in this passage: "there is properly no history; only biography." Other readers have confessed, as I do here, to supposing that by "biography" Emerson really means "autobiography," a word coined in the first decade of the nineteenth century. Has he not just finished saying that "all history becomes subjective"? Again I suspect that he intends to generate confusion. He wants to bewilder us into assenting to the proposition that indeed autobiography, if you assiduously dig into it, soon enough becomes the biography of everyone else. Thus the Emersonian wit of Stein's title *Everybody's Autobiography*.

The most crucial sentences in this passage, and perhaps in the whole essay, have to do with "formula or rule," a variant of what he means by "circles" in the essay of that name:

> Every mind must know the whole lesson for itself—must go over the whole ground. What it does not see, what it does not live, it will not know. What the former age epitomized into a formula or rule for manipular convenience, it will lose all the good of verifying for itself, by means of the wall of that rule. Somewhere, sometime, it

will demand and find compensation for that loss by doing the work itself.

By the fourth sentence the word "it," which refers repeatedly to "mind," is suddenly and without warning referring to the "former age." That is, not only mind but the former age demands "compensation" for losses. This confusion as to reference is, again, meant to stand as a representation of reality. It suggests that simultaneously the mind is *in* the age, the age *in* the mind. Neither can locate an external point from which better to understand itself or, therefore, the other. "The field," he says in "Circles," "cannot well be seen from within the field." He is telling us something which everyone, of late, has heard many times over: that the mind gets to know itself in any age only through those media—here called rules or formulas—by which the age itself has been endowed with a sense of its own unique reality, its conventions as to "facts." To rid themselves of the continuing oppressiveness of these "facts," people of a later age must work back *into* the very processes by which, in the earlier one, the "facts" were created in the first place, by rules and formulas only contingent to begin with.

The effort required to do this is little different, it would seem, from the best efforts to read a poem or novel. By dint of such effort, the human mind comes gradually to understand that facts, previously taken for granted as such, are instead recognizably fictions. This can be a chastening discovery: it requires us to see also that in the present operations of our own minds, and in our own inventions of rules and formulas, we are subject to the same kinds of loss—of truth, of perceived reality, of energy—as those incurred by the mind in any earlier age. If the present age knows more than did the past one, then, to return again to Eliot's "Tradition and the Individual Talent," it is the past which it knows. Emerson is properly vague about the later time and place where the losses of the past must be compensated for—"somewhere, sometime." No particular age, no particular nation or continent is privileged in this respect.

Far from suggesting that we work our way into the past so as to recognize its otherness, he is saying that the effort forces upon us a recognition of likeness, of participation in past productions, however monstrous these may be. We are asked to seek out the burden that makes Melville's Ahab complain that he is "heaped" by the past. A few paragraphs further on, Emerson remarks that "A Gothic cathedral affirms that it was done by us, and not done by us. Surely it was by man, but we find it not in our man." We find it in "our man" only when "we apply ourselves to the history of its production."

It is not the past which is "wild" or "savage"; it is our need to think so. "All inquiry into antiquity,—all curiosity respecting the Pyramids, the excavated cities . . . is the desire to do away this wild, savage, and preposterous There or Then, and introduce in its place the Here and the Now."[14] "Belzoni," he writes, referring to the Italian archaeologist of the early nineteenth century, "digs and measures in the mummy-pits and pyramids of Thebes until he can see the end of the difference between the monstrous work and himself." "Monstrous" means huge and fabulously horrible. The word also has connotations of portent and warning, as if an ancient culture into which we "dig" only to find ourselves (a bit like Frost in "Directive") then points ahead into our own culture, and toward the economic edifices of the present that have also been built upon slave labor and human sacrifice. Belzoni's work is deconstructive only provisionally, so that he may ultimately recognize his and our participation in the constructions of "monstrous work."

It is at this point that another question for Emersonian pragmatists becomes essential and inevitable: if an understanding of the past consists not in reverence for its products but in a more active discovery of "the history of its productions," how then may that knowledge be used to make life better, now and in the future, a future to which Emerson and Whitman, James and Stevens so often seem to be speaking? Indeed, Emerson, Whitman, and Stevens explicitly invoke generations yet unborn as their ideal readers. Obviously, any of the strenuous work with language that eventuates in the writing and the reading of poems can substantially enhance an understanding of the past and of the relations to it of the present generation. Similarly, it is easy enough for a trained reader to show how poets "dig" into and "measure" the language they inherit and how this digging and measuring is the precondition of any effort to renew language, to trope, turn, transform it for the benefit of readers and writers, present and future. When Frost ends his poem "Mowing" with the lines "The fact is the sweetest dream that labor knows. / My long scythe whispered and left the hay to make," he manages, by being profoundly Emersonian, to combine a Yankee aphorism about putting something away for the future—"Make hay while the sun shines"—with a lovely conceit about poetic transmission under the "sun" of literary influence. Although, as Sidney admits, that sun can burn the brain, in Frost its effects are beneficent and loving. The mower in his "Tuft of Flowers," for instance, leaves his poems, his makings, as a sign to other poets who come to the work after him. The prevailing mood with respect to the past is, once again, comradely, and results in poetry that is often surpassingly beautiful and expectant.

•

Emersonian pragmatists, however, in their repeated suggestion that the work of philosophy and poetry is a real part of the work of the world, promise more than the production of future generations of poets and poems. With different degrees of confidence, they promise to help effect transformations not just in writing, but in the actual forms of individual and communal life. While Emerson, James, and their poetic successors would agree with Eliot when he says art changes but "art never improves," their rhetoric, unlike his, is mostly in a socially optative mood. We need not, should not, be satisfied, they imply, with any equivalent statement about social institutions—that social institutions change but never improve.[15]

On this score Emerson seems to me the most troubled of these writers, the most uncertain, and with the rare courage of an uncertainty that will at all costs speak its mind. Believing, as he says in the Journals for August 1847, that "Life consists in what a man is thinking of all day," he must therefore admit to the worst as it happens to him, as well as to the best, and, if he is truly optimistic, be willing to say the worst and trust to its being overridden. He *takes on* more trouble for us than do any of his inheritors. He is troubled in his sentences, which so often give way to doubt; he goes to the trouble everywhere of wondering how good his sentences can be for himself or for anyone else. Without enunciating it as a policy, he tries hard to persuade himself, and us, that the kind of work that goes on in writing might change the way we manage our inheritance of language to a point where it might also change our habits of thinking.

And yet, as in "Self-Reliance," "The Conservative," or "New England Reformers," he is more careful than James not to confuse linguistic work of this nature with other kinds of work intended more directly to modify inherited forms of violence and repression. He never spoke more violently or came closer to violent altercations with his auditors, than when he took to the stump in an abolitionist fury of opposition to the speeches given in defense of the Fugitive Slave Law by his utterly failed hero Daniel Webster. In his attacks on Webster, Chapman remarks, Emerson is "savage, destructive, personal, bent on death." And yet he admits in his Journals for August 1852 that the work he is best suited to do, which are his lectures and essays, can address the plight of actual slaves only as part of his obsession with the less remediable enslavements of the human mind:

> I waked at night, & bemoaned myself, because I had not thrown myself into this deplorable question of Slavery, which seems to want nothing so much as a few assured voices. But then, in hours of sanity, I recover myself, & say, God must govern his own world, & knows his way out of this pit, without my desertion of my post, which has none to guard it but me. I have quite other slaves to

free than those negroes, to wit, imprisoned spirits, imprisoned thoughts, far back in the brain of man—far
retired in the heaven of invention, &, which, important
to the republic of Man, have no watchman, or lover, or
defender, but I.

The thoughts he wants to liberate are deeply buried, even
in the revered Shakespeare, from whose *Henry V* he silently
borrows the phrase "the heaven of invention."

William James, by contrast, tends to be jaunty about the
possible adaptation to the reform of social institutions of
those liberating efforts that work well enough, meanwhile,
on the page. In "The Moral Equivalent of War," the monograph of 1910 that won him more popular acclaim than
anything else he wrote, he frames a proposal explicitly designed to create a form in which it would be possible for
the entire community to trope or change a "monstrous
work" of the past, a work that seems permanently fixed—
war and the glorification of the martial spirit.[16] Being a
good Emersonian, he concedes that the responsibility for
this "monstrous work" is something we share with our
ancestors; it cannot be treated merely as a relic. Only the
most jingoistic American patriots could have refused to
recognize the monstrosity of war during a decade that began with the Spanish-American War and with American
atrocities in the Philippines. In part because of these events,
which in 1902 led to his joining the Anti-Imperialist League
of New England, of which he was for a time vice-president,
James became persuaded that war and the aura of military
exploit were essential parts of "the romance of history," and
that since the romance could not be repressed it had best

be rewritten into something more prosaic and more socially beneficial.

In an appealing exercise of Emersonian complicity, he argues that pacifists ignore the aesthetic and even moral attractions of war. These include the glamour of uniforms, the incitements to sacrifice and comradeship, all the things by which the war party wins approval from the rest of the community. That community is unwilling, he says, to "envisage a future in which army-life, with its many elements of charm, shall be forever impossible, and in which the destinies of peoples shall nevermore be decided quickly, thrillingly, and tragically, by force, but only gradually and insipidly by 'evolution.'" Nor will it do to point to the expenses and horror of war. "The horror makes the thrill," he observes, "and when the question is of getting the extremist and supremest out of human nature, talk of expense sounds ignominious."

Since war apparently expresses an unquenchable human need and is, besides, "the only force that can discipline an entire community," James decides to treat it like a literary metaphor that needs to be troped. He decides that what is required is an equivalent to war. To be effective, this equivalent will have to satisfy the needs that lead to war in the first place, without entailing bloodshed. His proposal, which came to fruition of a sort in the Civilian Conservation Corps of Franklin D. Roosevelt and the Peace Corps of John F. Kennedy, is that there should be "a conscription of the whole youthful population to form for a certain number of years a part of the army"—and I call attention to the next phrase—"enlisted against *Nature*." Everyone, he stipulates, especially our "gilded youths," would be sent into "coal and iron mines, to freight trains, to fishing fleets in December." They would be required to wash dishes, wash clothes, wash windows.

"The Moral Equivalent of War" provides the one occasion when James is criticized, according to Jo Ann Boydston, in the voluminous letters of his younger admirer at the University of Chicago, John Dewey. Writing to Scudder Klyce in 1915, Dewey complains that James's essay

> seemed to me to show that even his sympathies were limited by his experience; the idea that most people need any substitute for fighting for life, or that they have to have life made artificially hard for them in order to keep up their battling nerve, could come only from a man who was brought up an aristocrat and who had lived a sheltered existence. I think he had no real intimation that the "labor problem" has always been for the great mass of people a much harder fight than any war; in fact one reason people are so ready to fight is the fact that that is so much easier than their ordinary existence.[17]

In defense of James here, it could be said that Dewey fails to take sufficiently into account the clear indications in the essay that there is a distinction to be drawn between two kinds of work. One kind, which James has in mind for his conscripts, is formed, shaped, and intended as a shared discipline. The other, evoked in Dewey's letter, is work which Dewey elsewhere associates with drudgery for the satisfactions of economic need. Curiously enough, Dewey had just made these distinctions himself in *Democracy and Education,* a book published the very year the letter was written. In terms that confirm his allegiances to Emerson,

Dewey speaks unfavorably of "work" when it is a mere "subordination of activity to an ulterior material result," and he goes on, glowingly, to describe another kind of work. He says of it that "Like play, it signifies purposeful activity and differs *not* in that activity is subordinated to an external result, but in the fact that a longer course of activity is occasioned by the idea of a result." Dewey's "idea of a result" is a version, it seems fair to say, of James's "practical cash-value," and it seems obvious, too, that this is exactly the kind of work which James wants to make into "a moral equivalent of war."

James's proposal is in fact more simplistic in its conception and more insidious in its effect than Dewey makes out. Its simplification consists in supposing that war results from militaristic sentiment, inbred pugnacity, or because war, as he puts it, "is the *strong* life." By that logic, ordinary folk not only fight the wars, they plan and start them. As if popular sentiment or feeling, rather than the calculations of Theodore Roosevelt as Under-Secretary of the Navy, so arranged things that the American fleet had already been assembled within striking distance of Manila weeks before the Spanish-American War was precipitated by the still mysterious sinking of the battleship *Maine* in Havana harbor. A war is not planned and started by youths who have yet to attend his work camps. It is, as Clausewitz had argued nearly eighty years before James's essay, a political act, and, even more, "simply a continuation of political intercourse, with the addition of other means." Because he refuses any such acknowledgment of politics, James must find his causes for bellicosity elsewhere, in something called "nature" and in something called "life."

It is here that the effect of his essay is most insidious. His youths need something to work against, but the opponent must at any cost *not* be a political one. Youth needs to be taught a lesson always dear to Emersonian pragmatists, the lesson that, as John F. Kennedy put it, "life is unfair." Don't blame it on institutions, blame it on life or, in James's capitalized term, on "Nature." After him, Frost will say "war is the natural state of man" and, before him, Emerson, in "Self-Reliance," had already issued the call: "let us enter the state of war."[18] Life *"feels* like a real fight," James says in "Is Life Worth Living," part of *The Will to Believe,* and it is evident that for him, as for the others, the enemy was nowhere and no one in particular. The enemy had no political, economic, social, or historical identity. Life *"feels* like a real fight" because it is "as if there were something really wild in the universe which we, with all our idealities and faithfulness, are needed to redeem."

James is not therefore saying, as Dewey alleges, that "most" people need a "substitute for fighting for life"; he is saying that *all* people need to be taught why and how they *must* fight for it. They cannot get to know this in the workplace, where the opponent might by some mischance become superficially localized as the boss or the owner. Only by moving them out of the workplace entirely can we be sure that our youth will recognize that the real enemy is called Nature, and that there is no other enemy, certainly not the social or economic system that sets the conditions for work.

James is not in the least conscious of having a political program here, much less of its deviousness. It simply never occurs to him that in America there can be any permanent, rooted enemy beyond whatever he means by Nature. What is perhaps most telling and disturbing is the ease with which "war" gets translated into "work," so that the opponent of work, no less than of war, is always external to America. The enemy is never within America's economic-social system, it is only whatever is opposed to America, even potentially. The mentality of the "moral equivalent of war" sounds dispiritingly like a preparation for the mentality of the Cold War.[19]

Though Dewey does not make an effective argument against James (nor was he obliged to do so in a letter), his instincts are nonetheless right. Joining with Emerson and Whitman on the one side and, on the other, Frost, Stein, and Stevens in their shared distaste for social or economic theory, James never asks, anymore than do they, why the inescapable hardness of life needs to be exacerbated by practices of economic and political organizations and networks. I cannot agree with Frank Lentricchia's otherwise admirable interpretations of James (and Dewey) when he suggests in *Criticism and Social Change* that James's anti-imperialism was even incipiently Marxist. This takes no account of Santayana's incisive ridicule of James in *Persons and Places,* where he recognized that during the Spanish-American War James was shocked less by imperialism than because America was not proving itself to be unique among the nations. According to Santayana, America was simply acting the way emerging great powers have always acted. James, he writes, "held a false moralistic view of history, attributing events to the conscious ideals and free will of individuals: whereas individuals, especially in governments, are creatures of circumstance and slaves to vested interests."[20]

Indeed, within a mere seven months of the signing of

the Treaty of Paris in February 1899, which delivered the Spanish empire to the United States, James is writing on September 11 to William Salter from Bad-Nauheim about the Dreyfus case as if America were in reality free of systems and institutions altogether, as if it were occupied only by individuals, a few noble ideas, and Nature, alternately seen as an ally or enemy. Such a notion may sound astoundingly naive to readers now, but its coherence with the very founding ideas of the republic has been brilliantly laid bare in Myra Jehlen's *American Incarnation*. The illusions in James's letter are still vitally a part of our imagination of ourselves as a nation. Having expressed his outrage that Dreyfus has once again been found guilty, he says, speaking of France, that "the breath of the nostrils of all these big institutions is crime—that is the long and short of it." He then turns with evident relief to his altogether exceptional New World:

> We must thank God for America; and hold fast to every advantage of our position. Talk about our corruption! It is a mere fly-speck of superficiality compared with the rooted and permanent forces of corruption that exist in the European states. The only serious permanent force of corruption in America is party spirit. All the other forces are shifting like the clouds, and have no partnerships with any permanently organized ideal. Millionaires and syndicates have their immediate cash to pay, but they have no intrenched prestige to work with, like the church sentiment, the army sentiment, the aristocracy and royalty sentiment, which here [in Europe] can be brought to bear in favor of every kind of individual and collective crime—appealing not only to the immediate pocket of the persons to be corrupted, but to the ideals

of their imagination as well. . . . My dear Mack, we "intellectuals" in America must all work to keep our precious birthright of individualism, and freedom from these institutions. *Every* great institution is perforce a means of corruption—whatever good it may also do. Only in the free personal relation is full ideality to be found.

"We 'intellectuals' in America must all work to keep our precious birthright of individualism, and freedom from these institutions." For all his epistolary charm, James can lend himself to vapid political rhetoric of this kind without its ever exciting in him that instinctive revulsion which in similar circumstances makes Emerson's prose, no matter how informal, suddenly bristle against itself with retaliatory puns, mordant allusions, and syntactical distortions. It is therefore James, of the two, who is apt to expose most glaringly some of the fault lines of Emersonian pragmatism. The word "work" as used in the letter is obviously idiomatic, and he is obliged by the occasion neither to specify its nature nor even to characterize it metaphorically. And yet his very casualness makes it all the more obvious that the "work" to which he summons Salter and other "intellectuals" is to be constructive only in the sense that it is preventive. It is meant to prevent existent texts, you might say, from calling our attention away from ongoing works. It is to prevent the emergence of forms and institutions in America which, in Europe, are "rooted and permanent" or propped up by "intrenched prestige." For James, nothing has so far been built into American history that obstructs the uninterrupted progress from past to future of "our precious birthright," nothing in the century and a quarter since the founding, though in conscience any American at the turn of the century might already have chosen to bear witness to the extermination of Indian tribes, the repeated cycle of market failures and the persistence of poverty, the persistence, too, despite the abolition of slavery, of apparently ineradicable racism—all these as giving evidence, perhaps, of some "permanent forces of corruption" in the American way of doing things. James's letter rhetorically flourishes a view that persists as a line of force in American life all the way from Emerson to Frost to the present decade. It is a view of the United States in which in fact there *is* no system; there is only Nature, and forces that are "shifting like the clouds."

All the while, however, there is one form or institution that for Emersonians always carries with it the absolutely inescapable taint of system and repressive inheritance. And that, of course, is language. Language is the one cultural infiltration from Europe that cannot be stopped, the one institution from which it is impossible ever to insulate the New World.

The proper activity envisioned from "intellectuals" is therefore essentially a poetic one. It is to make sure that language is kept in a state of continuous troping, turning, transforming, transfiguring, even to the point of transparency. Emerson had set the course in "Self-Reliance," when he asserted that "Power ceases in the instant of repose"; and he set the pace for that course when he added that power "resides in the moment of transition from a past to a new state." You will notice that "power" is not said to be a result of the transition; it is said rather to be *in* it, and nowhere else. Power, work, the self—all of these achieve a mutual and simultaneous realization in those momentary fusions when agent, act, and instrumentality (meaning words) find that they are as one. This means also that each discovers at that moment an inconvenient dependency on the others, and a disconcerting necessity, therefore, to move on to the next transition, toward a similar but again only temporary fusion.

This imagination of work, power, and self is, insofar as I can describe it, indistinguishable from what is imagined by these same writers as the ideal operation of writing and reading, the operation by which a poem is created. And even a poem, according to Frost, is only a "momentary stay against confusion." Frost shows here his laconic elegance in the face of a very chilling aesthetic.

To summarize just a bit: Work for Emersonian pragmatists has become a mode of action by which an inheritance, instead of being preserved or reverentially used in the present, is radically transformed into a bequest for the future. "Truth," says James in "Pragmatism's Conception of Truth," means in most circumstances "nothing but eventual verification." While these writers may vary markedly in tone and emphasis one from another, it is noticeable that none ever misses an opportunity to insist that his or her own writing, even as it emerges on the page, is the epitome of what work can best accomplish. Thus Emerson, in the first section of his first book, *Nature,* instructs neighboring farmers that he, and not they, can claim the landscape: "There is a property in the horizon which no man has but he whose eye can integrate all the parts, that is, the poet." Thus Thoreau proposes that "some must work in fields if only . . . to serve a parable-maker one day," and Whitman, in "Song of the Broad-Axe," celebrates the cutting down of ancient forests for the glory of America conceived as a poem-in-progress, preparing the way for his admirer James, who characterizes philosophers and poets as "blazes made by the axe of the human intellect" on the "otherwise track-less forest of human experience."

Once war has been poeticized as "the *strong* life," it is easy enough to imagine an equivalent for it in the already deindustrialized work which Emersonian pragmatists have made into a species of poetry. A way is then open for a configuration in which war/work becomes a version of po-etic writing and reading, a version of "symbolic action" that embraces all other actions. It is in that light that one can read the heading of Burke's *A Grammar of Motives:* "ad bellum purificandum"—to purify warfare. When "war" gets turned into "work," then, it is not merely for the benefit of societies but as a metaphor, notably in Stein and Mailer, for literary composition, for the massing and deployment of literary resources. "It is quite certain," says Stein in "Composition as Explanation," "that nations not actively threatened are at least several generations behind themselves militarily so aesthetically they are more than several gener-ations behind themselves and it is very much too bad. . . ." Wallace Stevens, writing during World War II in the coda to *Notes Toward a Supreme Fiction,* makes the claim that the war, actually being fought by soldiers in Europe and Asia, is only a local engagement in the neverending war fought by poets like himself.[21] While allowing at least that "war for war, each has its gallant kind," he leaves no doubt where the greater effort and glory lies:

Soldier, there is a war between the mind
And sky, between thought and day and night. It is
For that the poet is always in the sun,

Patches the moon together in his room
To his Virgilian cadences, up down,
Up down. It is a war that never ends.

Of course the other war may end for the unfortunate
soldier when he gets killed, but we already know from an
earlier poem, "The Death of a Soldier," that when that
happens "The clouds go, nevertheless, / In their direction,"
a little like those "shifting clouds" in James. Such claims
for the work of the poet may strike you, according to your
mood, as extravagant or impertinent or amazing or exas-
perating or offensive. Then again, they might strike you as
simply true. So utterly indistinguishable, for me at least, is
this myth about poetry from myths about America, that to
some considerable extent any response to these exorbitant
claims for literary work will probably depend on your feelings at any given moment about America—both the idea
and the current embodiment of that idea in the United
States.

III

THE REINSTATEMENT OF THE VAGUE

While making a case for itself, Emersonian pragmatism, like other isms, depends on certain key, repeated terms. But to a wholly unusual degree it never allows any one of these terms to arrive at a precise or static definition. Their use is conducive less to clarification than to vagueness, as has already been shown with words like "action" and "turning," or "power" and "work," or "nature" and "privacy," along with words having to do with speaking, with trying in public to sound authentically like yourself. While some delimited understanding of these is necessarily assumed as a starting point, the dictionary will be of little help in determining how they function; they are no less figurative in the philosophic writings under consideration than are corollary uses in the poetry; they are constantly being troped within sentences that insist that readers, too, must involve themselves in the salutary activity of troping.

Why salutary? Because though troping involves only words, it might also, as an activity, make us less easily intimidated by them, by terminologies inherited from the historical past or currently employed in the directives of public policy. It might like any art prevent a society from "becoming too assertively, too hopelessly, itself," as Kenneth Burke phrased the possibility some sixty years ago in *Counter-Statement*. It might help us confront the authority, along with its ideological or gendered assumptions, invisibly structured into the customary orderings of sentences and paragraphs.

Thus, we have already heard James, in "what Pragmatism Means," enjoin us to "set [each word] at work within the stream of your experience." The word will then be recognized "less as a solution . . . than as a program for more work." Though this is a worthy enough injunction, it is compounded of terminological blurrings that could easily make anyone unsure of just how and where to carry it out. It would be helpful to know, for example, where this stream of experience is located before we begin to set a word at work within it. Is the stream in us? Or is it shared with others? Are we on it, or is it next to us? In any case, how is one to identify the stream as peculiar to oneself—and how are its movements to be traced without the use of words, words that will inevitably mediate and thus contaminate or redirect the stream's flow? What, besides, can be meant by the word "work"? In the next sentence all he can promise is that if we set the word "at work within the stream," we will discover "a program for more work." But this work will produce nothing beyond an "indication"— an "indication of the way existing realities might be *changed*."

The italicizing of the word "changed" is one of several signs of James's anxiety lest we wonder what the urgency and effort really accomplish after all. The blurring and vagueness in his formulations are a rhetorical effort to persuade us, and himself, that the "work" will indeed amount to more than a poetic exercise of troping or changing. In fact, however, we cannot even begin to know beyond that where any change is to occur or who will be helped by it. Will it, for example, benefit the millions who haven't the capacity or opportunity to read James's sentences? The change, as he describes it, can at most be a change in some word or other, some word which has, to begin with, a very tentative hold on the "realities" to which he refers. As I see it, he offers here a prescription and a promise only for the writing of poetry and prose. And while these may on occasion change the perception of reality by a particular reader, James's rhetoric, like Emerson's, is obviously hinting at more consequential rewards.

I mean to suggest that James's language is no less "superfluous," in the various senses attached to that word, than is the language of the poets I have allied with him; it is subject to the same degree of metaphorical proliferation, slippage, and excess. James's predecessor Emerson is the more "superfluous" of the two, offering a surplus of meaning in the face of always incipient impoverishment, but James's writing is also "extravagant" and "extra-vagant," writing in which language moves out of bounds, toward the margin, until it becomes loose and vague. Emerson intends to go, as it were, beyond us, and for the reason that, like James—though in a style far more calculated, conscientious, and entangled—he admits that he is writing for the future and into the future. However, he came increasingly to acknowledge that this future might forever elude all the human generations, as is poignantly suggested by those verbs of postponement that lift up even as they deflate the final sentence of "Experience": "the true romance which the world exists to realize, will be the transformation of genius into practical power." Don't hold your breath, is what he is saying. If pragmatism works, then it works the way poetry does—by effecting a change of language, a change carried out entirely *within* language, and for the benefit of those destined to inherit the language. Pragmatism, as I understand it, is not essentially addressed to—indeed it shies away from—historical crises, real or concocted.

This relative indifference to crises, to any cultural apocalypse, helps explain, I suspect, why writers of an Emersonian pragmatist disposition were, for the most part, ignored or regarded as insular and pleasantly irrelevant during the period from about 1920 to 1960. This was a period when the wasteland ethos, with its admixtures of Anglo-Catholicism and Southern Agrarianism, dominated the American literary-academic scene, far more, it should be remembered, than it did the English one. Frost, Stein, and Stevens, not to mention their nineteenth-century predecessors, were generally patronized by the higher criticism for having failed—and what a creditable failure it was!—to subscribe to Eliot's rhetoric about the twentieth century, this "immense panorama of futility and anarchy which is contemporary history," as he described it in the 1923 essay *"Ulysses, Order and Myth."* Frost seems obviously to have had such a characterization in mind when, in 1935, he dryly remarked in a letter to *The Amherst Student,* an undergraduate newspaper, "It is immodest of a man to think of himself as going down before the worst forces ever mobilized by God."

I have already made detailed arguments in *The Renewal of Literature* against the literary and cultural distortions brought on by the acceptance as historical reality of Eliot's idiosyncratic mythologies of twentieth-century crisis and of a consequent obligation, as he saw it, to write a "difficult" and "allusive" poetry like Eliot's own. The Emersonian pragmatist counterview is that there cannot be a crisis of authority which is not also the occasion for celebration and release. As they would have it, the past, including the literature of the past, proves that crisis and celebration are a mixture inherent in human nature. Human consciousness, so their account of it would run, is itself an invention which mediates both the imagination of freedom and the ever-haunting sense that freedom is what we have sacrificed to consciousness. The invention of consciousness is simultaneous with the invention of language, which, in turn, measures both the restraint upon and the expression of human freedom. For all practical purposes, human beings are constituted by language; they exist in it, and also by means of it. "It is very unhappy, but too late to be helped," Emerson calmly remarks in "Experience," "the discovery we have made, that we exist. That discovery is called the Fall of Man. Ever afterwards, we suspect our instruments."

Complaints about these "instruments"—what Santayana calls "the kindly infidelities of language"—can be heard as far back as the debate in Plato's dialogue of Cratylus and on through Augustine, Bacon, and Locke. What worries even while it excites Emersonian pragmatists is the actual *inadequacy* of language to the task of representing reality. This becomes a determining factor in their understanding of the work required by writing and by reading. Even before Emerson, such concerns were voiced in America by Jonathan Edwards,[1] along with his resolution of them, and after Emerson in Stevens's suave acceptance of the fact, as in his poem "The Creations of Sound," that "speech is not dirty silence / Clarified. It is silence made still dirtier."

A question that inevitably needs to be asked is why an

age-old skepticism about language should have become so pronounced, should so frequently emerge as the inferable subject of Emersonian pragmatist writing. Perhaps more important still is the question of why, nonetheless, the tone of that writing hints at so few of the grim cultural prognoses heard not only in Eliot but in more recent complaints that language is a prison-house, an instrument of repression that destroys individual identity even as it bestows it.

Having posed these questions, let me try to answer them. For Emersonian pragmatists, as I read them, language becomes the surrogate for all other forms of institutional and systematic power; it becomes a substitute for what Emerson calls Fate, and an evidence of the unappeasable human need to blame *something* for our always being less than we intend to become. The geographical literalization of the European mythology of a New World, which Myra Jehlen has convincingly traced out, induced in American writers the conviction that the North American continent is blessedly free of those institutional corruptions that will forever infect the old. And yet, in many cases, an occupational hazard of being an American writer simultaneously compelled another conviction: that language itself remained the one unavoidable cultural inheritance, the one forever demanding Old World institution, that could not be dispensed with. However, a felt need to dispense with it became, for those of an Emersonian inclination, unremitting, not to be assuaged even when you might leave your study, divest yourself of books and of family, and all by yourself go, as Emerson notoriously says he did, to the bare common in Concord, there to become for a brief moment a transparent eyeball. Why even then was it not possible to escape from language? Because it remained the necessary medium by which to talk about efforts to get out of it or beyond it. Language thus came to embody whatever it was that stood in the way of transparency, of the desire—closer to realization on this allegedly bare common of a New World than anywhere else—for an unimpeded expression of human power.

It could be said, then, that insofar as America is represented by Emersonian pragmatists it has always been what is called postmodernist. That is, Emerson's America is a place that from the outset recognized the contingency of all institutions and recognized language as a form of knowledge that was also a form of repressive power. But where Emersonian pragmatism veers away from this postmodernism is in its belief that language, and therefore thinking, can be changed by an individual's acts of imagination and by an individual's manipulation of words. Pragmatism, especially the Emersonian-Jamesian version, seems to me essentially a poetic theory, and while it could therefore be said to evade philosophy (as Cornel West and Harold Bloom, on other grounds, say that it does) I think this is to take a too circumscribed view of what it means to write philosophy. I would tilt the issue somewhat differently, by arguing that Emerson and, to a lesser extent, James refuse systematically to inveigh against the conceptual terminologies to which they are opposed because they know that in working out any such oppositions they would inevitably end up contriving only another terminology, and one no less abstract and potentially just as oppressive. They might get credit for staging a revolution in philosophy, but it would in their eyes be little more than a coup d'état, wherein some "power-bringing words" would be deposed only so as to allow others to appear on the balcony.

Quite prudently, therefore, they elected to stick with already familiar and nonprofessional forms of language. They did so on the assumption that what James says of beliefs is even more the case with words—that "at any time," as he maintains in "Pragmatism's Conception of Truth," they "are themselves parts of the sum total of the world's experience, and become matter, therefore, for the next day's funding operations." Familiar, homey words cannot, then, be dispensed with; they can, however, be reshaped, especially by alterations in any written syntax designed to catch those tones or sounds of speech that can substantially inflect or even reverse the meanings normally assigned to the words. We must learn once again to hear sounds already deeply embedded in the caves of the human mouth and of the human ear. Such sounds have been relegated by philosophers and intellectualists to the inessential, to the fringes of human discourse, and it is time, James concludes, to restore them to centrality. Thus, to paraphrase a passage of his, instead of focusing on ideas as signaled by nouns in sentences or by images in a poem, there is to be a compensatory emphasis given to transitives—verbs, adverbs, prepositions, conjunctions, and the like—to all the words which are usually assigned the lowly task of moving us toward the substantives and, once that has been accomplished, retiring to the kitchen. Or, to change the figure, rather than complaining, with that failed Jesuit Stephen Dedalus, about "the aquacity of language," you should, with Pater, Stephen's rejected angel, welcome it, remembering that, before Pater, Emerson had advised that "all symbols are fluxional."[2]

This image of flow is picked up in James's various images of streams. The implication is that the stability of words is achieved only in their fluid relations to other words, and that these are set in motion by the person using the words. So that however much can be learned from deconstructive readings about the instabilities of language, Emersonian pragmatists go beyond that to show how words may be kept in motion by human agency, and that their significance is to be found *in* that more or less calculated motion. Because we assent to the fact that instability adheres to language, we become aware, however, that any exertions of authority over it, even when so tentative as these, can be only temporary and sporadic.

The best way to recognize these exertions, these evidences of human presence, is by learning to listen for them, in prose all as attentively as in poetry. We should listen to writing the way we listen caringly to one another in conversation, often catching more from the sounds we hear in the movements of sentences, or fragments of sentences, than from the actual words. This sort of listening is what Frost had in mind in those letters of 1913 and 1914 in which he takes credit for inventing a theory he called "sentence sounds" or "the sound of sense." We often guess what is being meant, he claims, writing to John Bartlett on July 4, 1913, not from words but from "the abstract sound of sense," as "from voices behind a door that cuts off the words." Or later, again to Bartlett, on February 22, 1914, "a sentence is a sound in itself on which other sounds called words may be strung." In what follows, I prefer, with Frost, to talk about "sound" rather than about "voice," because the idea of voice tends to suggest that the human presence in *words* is more emphatic than anything allowed by sounds. Though the sounds I will be describing may be casual and crafty, that does not keep them from being very often prelinguistic.

I think that the incentive, perhaps the actual source of Frost's theory of sound is to be found in a passage in the chapter of James's *Principles of Psychology* entitled "The Stream of Thought":

> The truth is that large tracts of human speech are nothing but *signs of direction* in thought, of which direction we nevertheless have an acutely discriminative sense, though no definite sensorial image plays any part in it whatsoever. Sensorial images are stable psychic facts; we can hold them still and look at them as long as we like. These bare images of logical movement, on the contrary, are psychic transitions, always on the wing, so to speak, and not to be glimpsed except in flight. Their function is to lead from one set of images to another. As they pass, we feel both the waxing and the waning images in a way altogether peculiar and a way quite different from the way of their full presence. If we try to hold fast the feeling of direction, the full presence comes and the feeling of direction is lost. The blank verbal scheme of the logical movement gives us the fleeting sense of the movement as we read it, quite as well as does a rational sentence awakening definite imaginations by its words.

James's wariness about what he calls "full presence," as expressed in the penultimate sentence, is a version of Emerson's in "Self-Reliance," where a self in continuous transition is preferred to any self in repose; and James's approval in the last sentence of what he calls "the blank verbal scheme," looks ahead to Frost's Fourth of July letter to Bartlett, in which he refers to "the abstract vitality of our speech." It is, he says, "pure sound." Soon after this passage in "The Stream of Thought," and still more clearly anticipatory of Frost's theories, James remarks that "a reader incapable of understanding four ideas of the book he is reading aloud, can nevertheless read it with the most delicately modulated expression of intelligence." He then proceeds, and the italics are his, to talk about *feelings of tendency*—an echo of the phrase *"signs of direction"* used earlier—and says that these are "often so vague that we are unable to name them at all." It is at this point that he delivers the sentence from which I take the title of this chapter: "It is, in short, the reinstatement of the vague to its proper place in our mental life which I am so anxious to press on the attention."

Poetry has of course always depended upon vagueness as an effect of figuration, rhythm, rhyme, and meter. These are among the contrivances that have traditionally differentiated the rhetoric of poetry from the rhetoric of philosophy or physics. I am arguing, however, that the virtue and necessity of vagueness is brought forward by Emersonian pragmatists as an intellectual and poetic necessity, so that what has always been true of poetry and of poetic language is by them made generally so. This vagueness is a function of sound, of the way the inflected sound of words is manipulated so as to take the edge off words themselves, to blur and refract them. The sounds we will be attending to allow for the most easygoing sort of utterance, like the ambling dialogue of Melanctha and Jeff in Gertrude Stein's *Three Lives*.[3] It is as if the voice is idling, apparently not headed anywhere in particular. The sounds are often untranslatable into rational discourse, or are at least badly served by it. They insinuate an identity for the speaker without asserting one, since assertion depends for credence on dominant mythologies of self, particularly masculine mythologies. Shakespeare, a most androgynous writer, is in his plays obsessed with sound in the way in which I intend to use the term, not only because he meant his plays to be heard rather than read but because the idea of sound as a sign of barely enunciated presence is central to his thematics. *Antony and Cleopatra,* for instance, is essentially about two people who compete to be heard all through the play, even in his death scene at her tomb. "Let me speak a little," he says, still attempting a farewell address suitable to a Roman emperor. "No," she replies, "let me speak."

In citing Shakespeare I repeat my contention that the deconstructive drifts so natural to language can most conveniently (but not only) be traced in canonical texts, where they are exploited to the full. A canonical text, I would say, is generally one that does not want to clarify itself; a journalistic text is generally one that does. But this distinction must not be taken to mean that the deconstructive movements of language are unique to literature. If they were, how then would they be so audible to fans of Groucho Marx or Jackie Gleason's *The Honeymooners* or in the everyday talk of people closely allied in neighborhoods, in workplaces, and the like? Such ordinary people—and everyone is ordinary some good part of the time—are in fact immensely sophisticated about the mediating and mediated nature of words and phrases. Most of us talk all day and say nothing worth repeating or repeatable. "What did you two talk about?" "Oh, nothing!" It has mostly been sound, efforts to create the gel of human relationships, even as the gel is forever melting away.

Insensitivity to such ordinary uses of language is, I think, most conspicuous just where it should not be, for human as well as for scholarly reasons. I mean among professionalist members of literature departments who increasingly want to demonstrate that the study of literature has created a field of knowledge little different from a science, with its own chronologies of discovery and progress, and its own technical jargon, which has now become all by itself a subject of study. Literary language is indeed very different from ordinary language, but only as a matter of degree. The fallacy of thinking otherwise shows in a well-known remark by Paul de Man in *Blindness and Insight:* "the statement about language, that sign and meaning can never coincide, is what is precisely taken for granted in the kind of language we call literary. Literature, *unlike everyday language,* begins on the far side of this knowledge; it is the only form of language free from the fallacy of unmediated expression" (my emphasis).

De Man seems to me altogether mistaken in this instance. Of course literature can be said to know that it is mediated expression; so, however, can one's customary salutations in the morning. My platoon in the army consisted of fifteen or so teenagers; most had never finished high school; but when one would say to another "you son of a bitch" he would do so on the confident assumption that every one of his associates knew all about "the fallacy of unmediated expression." It matters not at all that no one of them would have been capable of manufacturing that phrase. Anyone who responded "don't you talk about my mother that way"—and only a few ever did—would have been put down as a numbskull. Obviously, "son of a bitch" is a phrase used all the time to mean anything except what it says, anything from "you're terrific" to "how about that!" Persons who use the phrase are not identifying themselves with the words, but wholly with the performance, with the tonal pitch that can be given to the words. That tone can indeed enunciate the charge that "your mother is a bitch," at which point the language game is usually over, and violence may ensue.

The "performing self" is a title I used as far back as 1971. In part I meant by it then, and mean by it now, a self that responds with a native guile to the deconstructive tendency in language. It responds less by assertion than by inflection. Counteraction would be too strong a word to describe the process. Indeed, the sounds in question would normally assist deconstructive movement. What I am proposing, however, is that the sounds are deployed so as actually to reverse that movement even while allowing it. We all hear these sounds every day, in the flow of familiar, sometimes scarcely audible phrases and words. They call little attention to themselves; they belong so naturally to the rhythm of human speech that everyone takes them for granted: "how about that"; "do you think so?"; "really?"; "well, I guess"; "sometimes I just don't know"; "maybe so"; all kinds of grunts and groans. Words like these tend to disappear on utterance, and are discounted. But in letting them pass unnoticed, it is likely that in our exchanges with one another we unintentionally suppress large areas of feeling and thinking.

In 1890, William James, in his first and greatest book, *Principles of Psychology,* made an argument against such suppression, even while its persistence led him to conclude early in the chapter on "The Stream of Thought" that "language works against our perception of the truth." This claim does not refer so much to words themselves. His stricture could scarcely exist without words; his and our perception of truth depend on them. He is referring rather to our habitual way of ordering them, to the way words "work" in sentences and paragraphs. It is in this, and not in trivial experiments with automatic writing, that his influence on Gertrude Stein shows to positive advantage. A bit later, for example, he says that "so inveterate has our habit become of recognizing the existence of the substantive parts" of the stream of experience that "language almost refuses to lend itself to any other use." That is, the structure of most sentences inclines us toward its conclusive terms or key words. He calls these "resting places," and he says their "peculiarity is that they can be held before the mind for an indefinite time, and contemplated without changing." Sound bites in political advertising depend upon using words in this way, with scarcely edifying results.

A convenient example of a substantive in poetry is the word "wall" in the opening line of Frost's poem "Mending Wall":

Something there is that doesn't love a wall,
That sends the frozen-ground-swell under it,
And spills the upper boulders in the sun;
And makes gaps even two can pass abreast.
The work of hunters is another thing:
I have come after them and made repair
Where they have left not one stone on a stone,
But they would have the rabbit out of hiding,
To please the yelping dogs. The gaps I mean,
No one has seen them made or heard them made,

But at spring mending-time we find them there.
I let my neighbor know beyond the hill;
And on a day we meet to walk the line
And set the wall between us once again.
We keep the wall between us as we go.
To each the boulders that have fallen to each.
And some are loaves and some so nearly balls
We have to use a spell to make them balance:
'Stay where you are until our backs are turned!'
We wear our fingers rough with handling them.
Oh, just another kind of outdoor game,
One on a side. It comes to little more:
There where it is we do not need the wall:
He is all pine and I am apple orchard.
My apple trees will never get across
And eat the cones under his pines, I tell him.
He only says, 'Good fences make good neighbors.'
Spring is the mischief in me, and I wonder
If I could put a notion in his head:
'*Why* do they make good neighbors? Isn't it
Where there are cows? But here there are no cows.
Before I built a wall I'd ask to know
What I was walling in or walling out,
And to whom I was like to give offense.
Something there is that doesn't love a wall,
That wants it down.' I could say, 'Elves' to him,
But it's not elves exactly, and I'd rather
He said it for himself. I see him there
Bringing a stone grasped firmly by the top
In each hand, like an old-stone savage armed.
He moves in darkness as it seems to me,
Not of woods only and the shade of trees.
He will not go behind his father's saying,

And he likes having thought of it so well
He says again, 'Good fences make good neighbors.'

Given the title of the poem, the first line seems naturally to focus on the idea of "walls" or "fences." Correspondingly, people tend to remember as its most famous line a cluster of substantives: "Good fences make good neighbors," wherein one substantive is said to generate the other. Like Emerson, however, Frost uses aphorisms—and this is clearly one of them—less to settle arguments than to muddy them. He resorts to a sort of shuffle, a movement that manages to scramble surrounding efforts at clarification. For example, the opening line begins as a series of dispersements—"something there is that doesn't love"—before it hits a blank "wall." "Something," "something there is"—these vague conjecturals can be heard throughout his poems. They have been heard before in "Mowing," where the speaker speculates of the whispering scythe that "perhaps" it was whispering "*something* about the heat of the sun, / *Something, perhaps,* about the lack of sound— / And that was why it whispered and did not speak" (my emphases). Or there is "For Once, Then, Something." Its very title indicates a willingness to celebrate not a gift of meaning but only an inconclusive promise of it.

Others taunt me with having knelt at well-curbs
Always wrong to the light, so never seeing
Deeper down in the well than where the water
Gives me back in a shining surface picture
Me myself in the summer heaven godlike
Looking out of a wreath of fern and cloud puffs.
Once, when trying with chin against a well-curb,

I discerned, as I thought, beyond the picture,
Through the picture, a something white, uncertain,
Something more of the depths—and then I lost it.
Water came to rebuke the too clear water.
One drop fell from a fern, and lo, a ripple
Shook whatever it was lay there at bottom,
Blurred it, blotted it out. What was that whiteness?
Truth? A pebble of quartz? For once, then, something.

The spot he discerns at the bottom of a well is not "truth"; it is not, like the whiteness in *Moby-Dick,* a visionary possibility; it does not claim to be a metaphor. It is called only "something." There are enticements to significance here; there are, however, no entitlements. It is by that particular phrase—"For once, then, something"—that one is held to so strict an accounting. The phrase refuses to surrender its vagueness to any one of a variety of competing emphases, which can fall on the word "once" or on the word "something" or, by different prolongations of voice, on "then." In its central image—the picturing of a human face in water—the poem enters into a dialogue with a procession of other works by other writers wherein individual identity gets elevated above its own reflected image so that it may then gaze down on itself as if it were, absurdly, looking into the source of life's mystery. For Frost, who probably knew more Greek and Latin than any of his poetic contemporaries, the echoes of Narcissus would go back to Ovid, and in English to Spenser and Milton, as John Hollander points out in *Melodious Guile* with respect to a similar image in Frost's "Spring Pools." Frost, an avid reader of Milton, knew the scene in Book 4 of *Paradise Lost* where Eve first discovers her image in a pool: "As I bent down to look, just opposite, / A shape within the wat'ry gleam appeared / Bending to look on me." The recurrence of this figuration in Frost is, however, uniquely comic, casual, shrugging. "Looking out of a wreath of fern and cloud puffs," he is clowning on Michelangelo's Sistine ceiling, and even though "that whiteness" evokes Melville's white whale, there is no hint here of the foreboding reference at the beginning of *Moby-Dick* to "that story of Narcissus" and "that same image we ourselves see in all rivers and oceans. It is the image of the ungraspable phantom of life." Coming closer to Frost's casualness, though with none of its self-mockery, is Whitman in "Crossing Brooklyn Ferry," reporting that he "Saw the reflection of the summer sky in the water, / Had my eyes dazzled by the shimmering track of beams, / Look'd at the fine centrifugal spokes of light round the shape of my head in the sunlit water."

More than his predecessors, Frost is playing around with the idea of reflection both as mirroring and—though less evidently than in "Spring Pools"—with reflection as thinking or discernment. Both kinds of reflection are "blurred" and "blotted" out by the simplest accident of water dropping on water. This figuration of blotting comes directly, I think, from Shelley's "To Jane: The Recollection," where reflections in a pool and in a mind suffer exactly the same fate as they do in Frost. But in Shelley the image is far more down-spirited than it is in Frost, who instead displays some of the quick impatience heard in "The Murders in the Rue Morgue," when Poe remarks that "there is such a thing as being too profound. Truth is not always in a well." Perhaps the closest approximation of Frost's attitude here occurs in *The Will to Believe,* where, in the chapter called

"The Sentiment of Rationality," James says that "The bottom of being is left logically opaque to us, as something which we simply come upon and find, and about which (if we wish to act) we should pause and wonder as little as possible." The opacity of the self in James and Frost provides no pretext for Melvillean bewilderments about "the ungraspable phantom of life." It is an occasion for easygoing self-caricature.

Sounds for Frost are the more significant when barely audible. In human speech this means that the sounds are so close to the uncalculated casualness of down-home talk as to incline us actually to inattention. The mysteries lurking in the vocabulary begin to get to you only when you force yourself to listen closely, and yet you trust so much in the sound that you barely listen at all. The implication is that we are brought together not by a shared commitment to explicitly defined values; we are brought together instead in a shared confidence that we are all somehow accommodated to what Stephen Dedalus in *Ulysses* calls "the ineluctable modality of the visible." That is, we really do not know what is there or cannot agree on what it is; and yet we assent, or so our most elementary idioms seem to indicate, to the fact that in life and in poetry there is "something" or only "something, perhaps." The value of such verbal sound is that, as pragmatism recommends, it points toward future realization, toward the existence of things which it cannot verbally re-present.

I have been suggesting all along that barriers to clarity can in themselves be modes of communication, expressions of human bonding.[4] The metaphors as well as the sounds of "Mending Wall" suggest as much, and the allegory of the poem allows for no distinction between language in poetry and language in daily life. "A curious formalization of the common speech" is John Peale Bishop's way of describing some similar if more pronounced achievements in Gertrude Stein. Frost is a great poet not in spite of his desire to be a popular one, as is sometimes suggested, but because of it. The desire is rooted in a perception of the mediated and poetic potentials of ordinary idioms. All of us live all the time with the fact that while the language of daily life creates structures we can believe in, it just as beneficially creates gaps in those structures, gaps in what it only pretends already to have settled.

Deconstructive and linguistic theories announce much the same conclusion with an air of discovery Frost would have found amusing. Like Emerson or James, Stein or Stevens, he thinks of the self pragmatically—it is "something which we come upon and find." Since that finding may quickly dissolve, we must be ready to move on to new findings. A deconstructionist argues that when a word is used as the sign of a thing it creates a sense of the thing's absence more than of its presence. This means, as if any good poet or sensible person has ever thought otherwise, that the word is not the thing it represents. Language, so the argument goes, can create an abyss—a Frostean gap with a vengeance—and writing is constructed on that abyss. Emersonian pragmatists like Frost or Stevens scarcely deny this, but for them the evidence of a gap or an abyss is an invitation simply to get moving and keep moving, to make a transition. (Harold Bloom's word "crossing" roughly approximates what I mean by transition, but is used to describe movements more abrupt and assertive than those I have in mind.)[5] A transition can patch over a gap with very indistinct and loose phrasings, the kind people habitually use without expecting that the phrases will do more than keep them in touch with themselves and others, all very noncommitally.

One virtue of the kind of sound I am describing is, then, that it can create spaces or gaps in ascertained structures of meaning and that it can do so in such a way as simultaneously to create trust and reassurance instead of human separation. The sounds invite us to live with others in a space of expectation rather than deferral, the space of "something, perhaps." That is the less than easy significance of "Mending Wall" insofar as it is a poem about the making of neighbors. And yet to be consistent with these sounds —not, again, any assertion the words make, but the *sound* of them—the poem never does or can directly yield all the significances I want to find in it. If Frost's "sound of sense" is to work as he said it could—through a door or a wall, so that particular words are inaudible—then some of that sense must remain obscure, untranslatable, and forever incipient, like Jamesian truth itself. The sound of the opening line of the poem, "Something there is that doesn't love a wall," creates a mystery, or what the poem itself calls a "gap." This gap is not filled by summary bits of wisdom, like "good fences make good neighbors," a line given, it should be remembered, to "an old-stone savage armed," as if aphorisms are crude weaponry. No, good neighbors are made by phrases whose incompleteness is the very sign of neighborliness: "something there is." Anyone can go along with that. The word "something" partakes mildly of the "mischief" attributed to the emergent energies of spring, when the frozen ground swell "makes gaps even two can pass abreast." It is the sort of "mischief" which creates chances for companionability; this "something" doesn't love walls; its love is given instead to the "gaps" in walls wherein people may join.

To rephrase the poem in Jamesian terms, the "old stone savage" can be called a believer in "substantives," like walls; the speaker of the poem, while not an enemy of substantives—it is he, after all, who invites his neighbor to join in mending the wall—puts his faith more in what James calls "transitives," in whatever moves things from static positions, be it the forces of spring or the activity of hunters. Naturally, he also wants to provoke motions of mind, and sets out therefore to challenge other people's verbal formulas, less by rejecting them outright than by tactful indirection: "I wonder / If I could put a notion in his head," or "I'd rather / He said it for himself."

In *Principles of Psychology* James complains, in effect, that sentences and paragraphs are usually structured so as to muffle the tonal modulations of speech, especially when these find their way into writing. While the pertinent passage in "The Stream of Thought" has become fairly well known, many of its own modulations have gone unheeded. It is usually read simply as a prescription for change, when instead it describes a situation which James knows probably cannot be changed: "We ought to say a feeling of *and,* a feeling of *if,* a feeling of *but,* and a feeling of *by,* quite as readily as we say a feeling of *blue* or a feeling of *cold.* Yet we do not: so inveterate has our habit become of recognizing the existence of the substantive parts alone, that language almost refuses to lend itself to any other use." He had just observed that "There is not a conjunction or a preposition, and hardly an adverbial phrase, syntactic form, or inflection of voice, in human speech, that does not express some shading or other of relation which we at some moment actually feel to exist between the larger objects of our thought. . . . the relations are numberless, and no existing language is capable of doing justice to all their shades." His strongest objection is reserved for a prevalent error in thinking which supposes that "where there is *no* name"—where there is only "something"—then "no entity can exist." And he concludes with a passage that is apt to make any of us feel guilty about the way we use language day by day: "All *dumb* or anonymous psychic states have, owing to this error, been coolly suppressed; or, if recognized at all, have been named after the substantive perception they led to, as thoughts 'about' this object or 'about' that, the stolid word *about* engulfing all their delicate idiosyncrasies in its monotonous sound."

James is partial to transitives and conjunctives, to fragments that decentralize any grammatical or "textual" structure and that loosen the gravitational pull of substantives. Even before *Principles of Psychology,* his writing looks for a grammar that will do the work of what he later called radical empiricism. The grammar would make us aware that the relations between things are as important to experience as are the things themselves. It is necessary to stay loose. His ideal grammar leads to his politics, and not the other way round. The grammar he proposes is already anti-imperialist, anti-patriarchal, while never becoming directly focused on political or social structures. It is at least implicitly feminist,

anticipating a passage in Gertrude Stein's extremely difficult
Patriarchal Poetry:[6]

> Reject rejoice rejuvenate rejuvenate rejoice
> reject rejoice rejuvenate reject rejuvenate
> reject rejoice.

Both in *Pragmatism* and in *The Meaning of Truth,* the rejection of logocentrisms, and the rejuvenations that go with
them, are articulated within confines having essentially to
do with language use. In his preface to the latter book he
argues that because "parts of experience hold together from
next to next by relations that are themselves parts of experience," the "directly apprehended universe needs . . . no
extraneous trans-empirical connective support, but possesses in its own right a concatenated or continuous structure." A structure so imagined need not ask for "a higher
unifying agency" like God, since its power derives from its
own internal movements. To repeat Emerson in "Self-Reliance," "power ceases in the instant of repose; it resides in
the moment of transition from a past to a new state."

James's pragmatism looks back to the two American
writers he most admired—Emerson with his transitions,
Whitman with his lolling about—and forward to Frost,
Stevens, and Stein. All three, along with Emerson and
Whitman, find in casual forms of speech a way to play
against the power of concepts or epistemic formations, and
yet each of them insists that the sounds thus produced have
a value in and by themselves. Individualism, as they represent it, is quietly eccentric; it refuses to adopt the tone
demanded of it by "the situation." It can withhold itself

from the over-defining appeals of ideologies, meanings, images, ideas that are making the rounds at any given moment. Such individualism can keep in touch with an idea without letting itself be possessed by it; it makes its presence felt, especially in the company of the more articulately opinionated, by a lot of Jamesian *and*s and *but*s, Frostean *something*s and *anything*s, by Stein's elaborately patterned repetitions and the many *as if*s[7] that frequent the poems of Stevens as well as Frost—not needing any help, by the way, from Hans Vaihinger, whose *Philosophy of As If*, published in German in 1911, was not available in English until 1924. The great human repertoire of muttering and murmuring gives irreducible tonal evidences of *someone* there who, in however tattered a shape, remains free floating of any fixed point. Such a presence cannot be deconstructed because the evidences of its self-definition are the sounds also of its self-abandonment as it moves on to other sounds or, as I am tempted to say, to "moving" sounds.

The American writers I have been discussing have made the value of sound explicitly a subject of their work, and explicitly a resource for eccentricity. They suggest that the individual voice has in fact little else to depend on beyond the sounds it makes and, decidedly, those it refuses to make. When, to recall an instance in "Self-Reliance," Emerson says that once anyone has "spoken with *éclat,* he is a committed person," he means, perhaps recalling some advice he had received earlier from his formidable aunt, Mary Moody Emerson,[8] that articulate speech will have made him a prisoner, "clapped into jail by his consciousness." The word "éclat" carries the root meaning of "splinter." By speaking emphatically you shatter and scatter, you lose rather than express your identity. This fear of the appropriating power of social discourse suggests that the American contingent anticipates an alliance with Nietzsche, Foucault, and Derrida, all differences among them allowed. And yet, it should be apparent by now that in pressing their case the Americans simply *sound* different. They sound altogether less rhetorically embattled, less culturally ambitious than do any of these European cousins.

Literary and cultural narratives that purport to account for the last two hundred years have uniformly neglected this central aspect of the Emersonian pragmatist contribution. I refer, again, to its laid-back, rather quiet way—if under an Emersonian more than a Melvillean dispensation —of imagining and responding to cultural crises. Those who write most confidently about some dubious sequence from a putative modernism to a putative postmodernism leave the American contingent from Emerson to William James on to Frost, Stein, and Stevens off the calendar altogether, as I have already suggested, choosing to locate the lines of force and development only among Continental figures.

Let me give an illustration. It has to do with the death of God, presumably in the late nineteenth century, and with the supposition that this brought about a unique depreciation in the authority of words and, necessarily, of the Word. However persuasive this argument sounds, it must be asked whether the death of God is to be imagined as a shocking discovery in some particular period, and therefore a good excuse for modernist literary anxiety with its anguish about the arbitrariness of language, or whether, instead, it has been a recurrent event to which at least some people have always been habituated and about which they can therefore talk with a certain calm. When Nietzsche announced the death of God in 1881 in *The Gay Science,* he had been assiduously reading Emerson. Indeed, he probably found his title for this book in a lecture called "Prospects," where Emerson says, of another European writer, "I am sorry to read the observation of M. De Tocqueville that a cloud always hangs on an American's brow. Least of all is it to be pardoned in the literary and speculative class. I hate the builders of dungeons in the air." (This is a figure Stevens would have admired, and an echo of it can in fact be heard in *Notes Toward a Supreme Fiction,* where he refers to "the celestial ennui of apartments / That sends us back to the first idea.") "We read," Emerson continues, "another commission in the cipher of nature: we were made for another office, professors of the Joyous Science."

Nietzsche could not have read an entry in the as yet unpublished Journals where Emerson refers, in July 1835, nearly fifty years before *The Gay Science,* to the death of God. I am not making the jingoistic claim that Emerson's obituary came first, especially since neither he nor Nietzsche has priority on that score. I point rather, and always, to the particular tone of voice in the writing, the particular sound in this case with which Emerson expresses the idea. He sounds as if it is something not at all remarkable, as if everyone already knows about it. The tone is easygoing, even jocular: "It seems as if every body was insane on one side & the Bible makes them as crazy as Bentham or Spurzheim or politics. The ethical doctrines of these theosophists are true & exalting, but straightway they run upon their Divine Transformation, the Death of God &c & become horn mad." Later, in 1868 (thirteen years before Nietzsche's), there is another such announcement, in a tone no less easygoing. This time it comes from William James. He writes to Oliver Wendell Holmes, in a letter from Dresden dated May 15, that "If God is dead or at least irrelevant, ditto everything pertaining to the 'Beyond.' " This looks ahead to "the remotest cleanliness of a heaven / That has expelled us and our images" in Stevens's *Notes,* even as it looks back to Emerson. James's "ditto" is a match for Emerson's "&c," and in both instances it is implied that you've heard all this before; you know the rest of the story.

The idea does indeed go far back. Most likely, Emerson would have remembered that at the beginning of the Christian era Plutarch, in "Why Oracles Cease to Give an Answer," reports that "great Pan is dead." Echoing this, while paraphrasing a passage in Jean Paul of 1796–97, Nerval says "God is dead! Heaven is empty—Weep, children, you no longer have a father." It is not necessary to know any of this beforehand, however, in order to recognize from the tone of Emerson and James that they took the idea to be a familiar one long before Nietzsche proposed it. How else could it have become so macabre a joke in Emily Dickinson, who imagines us finding ourselves on the right hand of God, only to discover that he no longer has one:

> Those—dying then,
> Knew where they went—
> They went to God's Right Hand—
> That Hand is amputated now
> And God cannot be found—
>
> The abdication of Belief
> Makes the Behavior small—

> Better an ignis fatuus
> Than no illume at all—

Historians of ideas can only be as good as their hearing. The best clue for determining how long an idea has been around is the way it is spoken about. Phrasing and pitch of voice will indicate, better than anything else, how familiar an idea has become in a given culture, its relative importance, and the possible reasons why it might, until its time had come, have been ignored. In this instance, the sounds made by Emerson, Dickinson and James, like some of the many comic rumblings in Stevens ("The death of one god is the death of all. / Let purple Phoebus lie in umber harvest, / Let Phoebus slumber and die in autumn umber") all indicate that God's reported demise is not as alarming or catastrophic for them as for others who are given to wastelandings. Keep cool but care, as a character in Pynchon advises. Emersonian pragmatists and pragmatist poets concern themselves more with God's aborning than with Gods aborting, and while Stevens's declaration that "the solar chariot is junk" protests too much, he means, more positively, that the disappearance of God permits a less obstructed chance actually to see the sun—which Emerson said most people do not see at all.

As some of the fragments quoted from Stevens might suggest—"the death of one God is the death of all" or "the solar chariot is junk"—his tone on this matter can be rather blustering, more defensively assertive than it is in Frost or James or even Emerson; far more so than in Stein. Of all of them he is the one most given to the extremes of oscillation between deprivation and creative ebullience, often in the same poem. Some of this probably registers those oscillations of sexual potency which are sometimes his inferable subject. But from testimony in his letters it appears to have had as much to do with feelings of spiritual emptiness and with doubts as to whether or not he could summon the creative energies required to dispel those feelings. Even while losing his early belief in the Christian God, he still maintained allegiances to Christian institutions, and there is evidence that at the end of his life he accepted instruction and baptism in the Roman Catholic faith. A comparable decision is unimaginable for Frost. With the death of the Christian God, Stevens was not be satisfied, as Frost was, by Jamesian hypotheses. If God has become a fiction then the only substitute for something so grand must be other supreme fictions, those of his own devising. As Milton Bates observes in *Wallace Stevens: A Mythology of Self,* he preferred fictions known to be untrue, and therefore liberating, to hypotheses which are simply unverified. "The final belief," according to an adage in *Opus Posthumous,* "is to believe in a fiction, which you know to be a fiction, there being nothing else. The exquisite truth is to know that it is a fiction and that you believe in it willingly."

When he gets round to discussing sound in poetry, it is with a rhetoric that magnifies its importance and its implications far beyond anything allowed by Frost with his "sound of sense" or by James with his desire to "reinstate" the vague, the inarticulate, the nameless "to their proper place in our mental life." Sound for Stevens becomes a supreme fiction, one that by implication has maintained its power more than have gods no longer with us. "And what about the sound of words?" he asks in the essay "The Noble Rider and the Sound of Words":

> What about nobility, of which the fortunes were to be a kind of test of the value of the poet? I do not know of anything that will appear to have suffered more from the passage of time than the music of poetry and that has suffered less. The deepening need for words to express our thoughts and feelings which, we are sure, are all the truth that we shall ever experience, having no illusions, makes us listen to words when we hear them, loving them and feeling them, makes us search the sound of them, for a finality, a perfection, an unalterable vibration, which it is only within the power of the acutest poet to give them. Those of us who may have been thinking of the path of poetry, those who understand that words are thoughts and not only our own thoughts but the thoughts of men and women ignorant of what it is that they are thinking, must be conscious of this: that above everything else, poetry is words; and that words, above everything else, are, in poetry, sounds.

Stevens' prose, as much as his poetry, asks for a good deal of pondering. It would be wrong to conclude, for example, that "the sound of words" is here given a position once occupied by God, as if it could ever achieve "a finality, a perfection, an unalterable vibration" traditionally ascribed to the unmoved mover. He is not proposing any Eliotic desire for a place of rest or fixity. Instead, he deifies the *activities* by which a sense of these things and a feeling for them might, on occasion and very rarely, be produced. This is within the power, he says, of only the "acutest poet"— "acutest" in the root sense of leaving a Jamesian mark—

and it produces a corresponding activity in us only because we are aware of a "deepening need." The need—inferentially for anything that might have the attributes of God—explains the imperative phrasing of "makes us listen . . . makes us search the sound" of words for the truth of "thoughts and feelings, which . . . are all the truth that we shall ever experience." Truth is not otherwise available. And yet, even to ask that "the sound of words" yield an "unalterable vibration" is to be far more ambitious for poetry than is Frost in "The Figure a Poem Makes," when he asks only that it yield "a momentary stay against confusion." It is also to invite the kind of despair about poetic creation more frequently heard in Stevens.

An especially beautiful example is the first section of "The Rock," entitled "Seventy Years Later":

It is an illusion that we were ever alive,
Lived in the houses of mothers, arranged ourselves
By our own motions in a freedom of air.

Regard the freedom of seventy years ago.
It is no longer air. The houses still stand,
Though they are rigid in rigid emptiness.

Even our shadows, their shadows, no longer remain.
The lives these lived in the mind are at an end.
They never were . . . The sounds of the guitar

Were not and are not. Absurd. The words spoken
Were not and are not. It is not to be believed.
The meeting at noon at the edge of the field seems like

An invention, an embrace between one desperate clod
And another in a fantastic consciousness,

In a queer assertion of humanity:

A theorem proposed between the two—
Two figures in a nature of the sun,
In the sun's design of its own happiness,

As if nothingness contained a métier,
A vital assumption, an impermanence
In its permanent cold, an illusion so desired

That the green leaves came and covered the high rock,
That the lilacs came and bloomed, like a blindness cleaned,
Exclaiming bright sight, as it was satisfied,

In a birth of sight. The blooming and the musk
Were being alive, an incessant being alive,
A particular of being, that gross universe.

There is a disturbing mixture here of directness with exploratory uncertainty, of forthrightness with confusion, a compulsion to speak along with a fear that there may be nothing to say. The personal laying bare finds itself in a vocabulary and syntax opaque even for Stevens, suggesting that a burden of obscurity is revealed to him in the very process of the poem's delivery to us. The aged poet is haunted by echoes of his earlier poetry and by the unreality of his life as that poetry now represents it to him. It could be said, to recall the passage just discussed from "The Noble Rider and the Sound of Words," that the recollected images no longer produce for him any semblances of reality or feeling because they lack the "unalterable vibration" of great poetry or the "finality and perfection" that would have assured them a kind of permanence. In effect, he is saying that his life of poetry is a failure. The mood recalls, as does this whole section of "The Rock," the opening paragraphs of Emerson's "Experience."

Partway through, he begins to react against this despairing view, though in so agitated a fashion as to suggest no ascertainable hope for recuperation. The past is and was an "invention," a "theorem," and his experiences now seem to have been "fantastic" and "queer." He has at this point begun to talk less about his poems in particular than about the spirit of poetry itself and to envision a creativity in which anyone, poet or not, may participate. The power evoked is impersonal, not exclusive to a specific time or place, not derivative of nature, much less God, who does not belong in the poem at all. The power depends for its credibility simply on the human need to believe in it, the belief being extemporized out of despair and attached to mere "blooming and musk." We are once again at the "bare rock" of Emerson's "Experience."⁹ The phrase "As if nothingness contained a métier" is doubly oxymoronic, both in Stevens's familiar use of "as if" and because of the obvious fact that "nothingness" contains nothing. To what can this "métier" refer, if not to a Jamesian will to believe *something*, to believe at least in the work of knowing? These conjectural movements do not validate the personal intensities or images of the past which the poet has tried to hold on to. Instead, they validate the possibilities for new invention, for making "descriptions," as James phrases it in "Pragmatism and Humanism," that may in themselves be "important additions to reality."

A lot depends in this reading on how one hears the phrase "it is not to be believed," along with the word "absurd." Harold Bloom's reading of this seems to me the inevitable one, as when he refers to their "bewildered, quasi-protesting urgency." So much so that the words are divested of anything so arch as the punning J. Hillis Miller finds in them. Like the words "something" or "anything" their meaning is entirely tonal. They do not make an argument beyond giving evidence of a human presence that refuses to be silenced; they are an impatient rejection of defeat amidst so many signs of defeat. Yeats's "Lapis Lazuli" is crossed here with Wordsworth's "Resolution and Independence."

One of Stevens's problems is that "human life," embodied in the poet and the figure he meets at the edge of the field, are not and could not, given their consciousness of loss and death, ever aspire to "an incessant being alive." Such being belongs only to "life" as a principle generally conceived, to something like James's "stream of life," or to the river of rivers in Connecticut, to recall Stevens's very late, very great poem of that name. It is a kind of life the two are able to invent as against the encroachments, on their own individual lives, of inevitable oblivion. "Two figures" could refer to lovers or to a husband and wife, of course, as Bloom supposes when he says that the poem represents a "humanizing struggle to imagine love." "Two figures" refers, still more agitatedly, I think, to the poet and his daemon, as in the dedicatory poem to *Notes Toward a Supreme Fiction,* where the pronoun "you," while apparently referring to Henry Church, refers instead to Stevens's muse. As already suggested, the word "two" ought not to encourage any mathematical pun on "surd" in "absurd." That would be far too contrived, too lucid, forced, and logical within the much greater thrust of anguish and exasperation in the poem. "Absurd" belongs quite desperately only to this speaker and cannot be taken from him by rummagings in the *OED*. Go with the sound, as one must do in equally confusing and resounding passages of Shakespeare, like those famous speeches in *Macbeth,* also responsive to the brutality of loss and time, the speeches beginning "tomorrow and tomorrow" and "pity, like a naked new-born babe / Striding the blast."

Such poetry eludes clarification; it exists in sounds that are right only for the occasion and are not to be abstracted in the service of other occasions. In that sense, Hillis Miller's reading of this part of the poem, in his chapter on Stevens in *The Linguistic Moment,* is antithetical to my own. It is a working out of some incipient possibilities in the language that seem to me already forsworn by more compellingly emotive and dramatic ones. Apropos the word "absurd" he writes:

> *Absurd*: from *ab,* away, an intensive here, and *surdus,* deaf, inaudible, insufferable to the ear. . . . A *surd* in mathematics is a sum containing one or more irrational roots of numbers. The square root of two is an irrational number. There is a square root of two, but it is not any number that can be said, rationally. A *surd* in phonetics is a voiceless sound, that is to say, a sound with no base in the vibration of the vocal chords. The original root of the word *surd, swer,* means to buzz or whisper, as in *susurration* or *swirl,* which I used above. The Latin *surdus* was chosen in medieval mathematics to translate an Arabic term that was itself a translation of the Greek *alogos*: speechless, wordless, inexpressible, irrational, groundless.[10]

By depriving "absurd" of voice and place—it could have the meanings Miller ascribes to it if it were relocated anywhere in the poem—this account makes the word "absurd" into an abstracted elucidation of the poet's disappearance, when it is instead an assertion, however merely guttural, of his refusal to disappear. The word is not to be taken as an analytic comment on the now soundless guitar; rather, it is in itself a human sound dredged up in opposition to the silencing of the guitar and of his bequest to poetry. And then, after saying further that the words of his poetry also "were not and are not," he makes yet another and similar counterassertion, "it is not to be believed." What then *is* to be believed? Again, only what he calls an "invention," a fiction, a product of the struggling will to believe in something beyond even human love or poetry.

As will have been noticed, perhaps, I have not been content merely to interpret this poem or to argue with other accounts of it. I am using the poem as an allegory of the kind of pragmatist reading that seems to me, quite aside from Wallace Stevens, important to human conduct. I want my readings of Stevens and of Frost or, on other occasions, of Stein, to be coherent with an American pragmatist heritage that goes back to Emerson, a philosophical heritage that is unique for the privileges it accords to casual, extemporized, ordinary idiom, to uses of language that translate into little more than sound. The sounds reveal human presences that barely manage, and only then by virtue of their unobtrusiveness, to frustrate any excluding, incipiently deconstructive forces that lurk in the more obdurate or, as James might say, intellectualist uses of words. Of course this heritage is also, to some extent, my own concoction, derived from an intense reading of Emerson, to whom I feel a deep personal obligation, and from an interpretation of James which makes him, though he never volunteers, into a philosopher of language. That is, I am doing what I feel temperamentally called upon to do, as is every other responsible reader.

Reading is nothing if it is not personal. It ought to get down ultimately to a struggle between what you want to make of a text and what it wants to make of itself and of you. The stakes do not seem to me much higher than that, even when a reader wants to show how a text carries within itself the enabling and sometimes discrediting structures of a surrounding political and oppressively gendered culture. Having over twenty years ago, especially in *The Performing Self*, paid my respects to the politics embedded in literary structures—a respect each generation must pay on its own terms—I am now bothered by something quite different, which can be called, perhaps crudely, the loud mouth of contemporary criticism. It can be traced back to the headiness of Eliot's modernism, as in his grandiose views of his own and of Joyce's practices, and it is evident in calls since then to speak loudly while carrying so delicate a stick as a novel or a poem. And while there is some healthy skepticism currently at work in criticism, especially as directed against literature's claims to transcendence or the incorporation of values, that skepticism needs also to be directed at the language of criticism itself and at *its* claims to large significance.[12] Literature, including criticism, exists in time, but fortunately it does not exist all of the time. Literature exists only when it is being read by someone, which is not often, not for long, and not by very many.

Maybe it is at most a stalling for time. I guess I admire Frost a bit more than Stevens, though such choices are tiresome, because he admits without any wringing of hands that a poem is only "a momentary stay against confusion." It is not he who says "only," since for him the moment is quite enough. I must say "only," however, because, in the profession to which I belong, momentariness is obviously too little to satisfy those who clamor, at the expense of literature, for so much more.

IV

READING PRAGMATICALLY
The Example of Hum 6

$\mathbf{A}$s books proliferate on the history of contemporary theory, so does the likelihood that most will eventually be consigned to the history of public relations. Their common theme is that every half-decade or so, since about 1960, new theories have been rushed into the perilous deadly breach of literary studies to rout older ones, by then ready for early retirement, or ideologically discredited, or just plain boring. Inexorably, according to a narrative now in vogue, we have moved from New Criticism to structuralism to post-structuralism, all thanks to "moves" among competing schools and masters. Literary departments of academia have never been able to plot achievements in their fields with the assurance vouchsafed departments of science, however illusory the assurance is, and they are easily persuaded by almost any scenario of alleged progress. These scenarios create reality rather than describe it, however, and do it by dint of conspicuous omissions. They are likely to ignore, for example, critical works of stunning individuality, like those of Empson or Blackmur, works written before the story of theory is now said to have begun, and predictive of many of its recent conclusions. And insofar as these histories touch upon the thorny subject of reading, they shy away also from evidence that some of the close linguistic analyses conducted in classrooms for several decades past were able to unearth the theories of language already deployed *within* literary works themselves, notably the canonical ones. Indeed, works tend to remain canonical, as Frank Kermode has argued, not because of their alleged dalliance with political or social stabilities, but because of their own linguistic instability, their tendency to slip their moorings and thus to encourage alternative interpretations, continually over time.[1]

While theory should not, of course, be confused with the fabrications of its annalists, and while the benefits of the one outweigh the distortions of the other, the balance between them is only perilously maintained. A theory, as apologists argue, comes into existence by asserting its capacity to make quite specific historical differences. Its laudable function is to create vantage points outside daily practice—particularly when practice presupposes, as it notoriously does in the United States, that it is innocent of politics—from which it can then show that such practice is itself necessarily governed by theories, however much it tries to shun them. In order to be politically or culturally efficacious, that is, theory, like the histories of it, must insistently point to and mark its progressive steps. Only by so doing can it inculcate that degree of self-consciousness and that redirection of effort which might redeem it from the frequent charge of professional opportunism.

But such balances as do exist between theory and the history of theory need to be asserted so as to avoid the sort of neglectful historicizing that slips into a review by Terry Eagleton in the *Times Literary Supplement* (November 24, 1989), where he remarks that "post-structuralist concern with the devious stratagems of language, not least with its ineradicably metaphorical nature, is cognate with the literary objects such criticism examines." It is unfortunate that Eagletons's guarded hospitality to canonical works of the past for their contribution to contemporary theory doesn't prompt a corresponding recognition about works of criticism written in the past. Instead, it seems to suggest that only with a French benchmark called "post-structuralism" was Anglo-American criticism alerted to a "concern with the devious stratagems of language." The term "poststructuralism" looks for its beginnings only to the year 1967, the publication date of Derrida's *De la grammatologie,* but all the term itself announces to me is some late conversions to a kind of linguistic skepticism, allied to pronounced theological and cultural skepticisms, already familiar to a number of readers and critics in England and the United States. As I have argued, a strong, particularly energizing mode of linguistic skepticism was already available to those who had learned to appreciate the distrusts of language implicit in the anti-foundationalism of Charles Peirce or William James or John Dewey, or who, even without exposure to these philosophers or to Santayana or Cavell, had otherwise come to appreciate the movements of language in Stein, Stevens, or Frost.

Without necessarily depending on any of these writers, however, certain kinds of intense close reading were being pedagogically advanced, well before the post–World War II period, which without defining themselves theoretically —at the time that would have been thought inappropriate in undergraduate classrooms—or calling themselves skeptical, managed to inculcate in more than a few teachers and students a habit of enjoying the way words undo and redo themselves to the benefit of social as well as literary practice.

This latter development was fairly frequent in the more enterprising small colleges, where intimate and intense workshop teaching most frequently occurs. On this occasion I have in mind my own experiences as an undergraduate after World War II at Amherst College and in an undergraduate course I later helped teach at Harvard called "Humanities 6: The Interpretation of Literature." Others have doubtless had comparable experiences; I am here speaking only of what I know best.

In telling the story of Hum 6 I want in part to help disrupt the calendar of theory and to loosen its intimidating hold. Along the way I hope also to show that the influences that passed through the course were American and English rather than European in origin, and that this had important consequences for its tone and character. Specifically, the influences included Emerson, Peirce, William James and John Dewey, Wittgenstein, Kenneth Burke, and F. R. Leavis, most of whom have been afforded little or no place in the history of contemporary theory. And I chose to print the piece in *Raritan Quarterly* because two of its editors who have had the most to do with setting the magazine's direction, Thomas Edwards and I, remain greatly affected by our roughly similar educational experiences as Amherst undergraduates and, later, as teachers in Hum 6. I am acutely aware in all my references to Amherst that the credit I give to Hum 6 at Harvard, and to its founder Reuben Brower, could be differently distributed so as to allow more prominence to some teachers at Amherst who were Brower's colleagues when he taught there, who initiated with him the parent courses of Hum 6, and who helped fashion many of the assignments used in the course after Brower started it at Harvard. Before long I hope someone will tell that fuller story, along with the story of Amherst English in general.

This piece began as a talk at a session of the Modern Language Association in December 1988, at which J. Hillis Miller and I were asked to discuss some problems of reading and their relation to criticism and pedagogy. I understood the topic to include the responsibilities to words which reading entails, an obligation to all the barely audible cultural inheritances carried within them. Reading can be a civilizing process, not because the meanings it gathers may be good for us—they may in fact sometimes be quite pernicious—but because that most demanding form of writing and reading called literature often asks us to acknowledge, in the twists and turns of its language, the presence of ancestral kin who cared deeply about what words were doing to them and what they might do in return. Traces of these earlier efforts make us aware, as few other things can, of the opportunities and limits of culture itself. Good reading and good writing are, first and last, lots of work. It was fitting, in that regard, that the papers the students were asked to write in Hum 6, in response to printed handouts of carefully phrased and detailed questions, were called "exercises." These exercises made reading an acutely meditative process without ever inviting anything so mechanical as the mere tracking of images.

One eventually gets beyond "exercises" of this kind, acquiring an easy and natural familiarity with the disciplines they instill, and yet any athlete or dancer or musician—or reader—must have learned *how* to exercise and when to get back to exercise in order always to know the rigors by which any degree of mastery is attained. Reading is an acquired talent with words, which is all that reading ever can be directly engaged with, and it involves the measured recognition that words can do unexpected and disturbing things to you. People who vocalize their reading, who let it register on the ear and not simply on the eye, are apt to be more than ordinarily sensitive to the fantastic and baffling variability of sounds in any sentence or phrase, and of how this precludes their arriving at any sure sense of meaning. The meaning of a piece of writing for them is in the perceived difficulty of securing one. If, as Wordsworth said in "Essay, Supplementary to the Preface" of 1815, the poet is "in the condition of Hannibal among the Alps, . . . called upon to clear and often to shape his own road," then it cannot be supposed, he later goes on to say, that "the reader can make progress of this kind, like an Indian prince or general—stretched on his palanquin, and borne by his slaves." Reading must be actively synchronized with the generative energies of writing itself. It is not enough to understand what is being said, since this is always less than what is being expressed.

Obviously, reading/writing of this kind cannot occur in space; it occurs in time, word by word, sentence by sentence, responsive to opportunities as they open up, to resistances as they are encountered, to entrapments which must be dodged, all of these latent in the words just previously laid down and in the forms, both large and small, that reading and writing often fall into. Reading, even more than writing, needs to be alert to these possibilities, if only because most writers cannot usually afford the degree of skepticism which is the privilege—some would say the obligation—of a reader. In that sense Shakespeare is the greatest writer of all time because he was also the greatest reader of his own words, never oblivious to their implications no matter how apparently at odds with his characterizations, never cheating on them even in the pursuit of theatrical spectacle or shapeliness, continuously renewing his words out of possibilities salvaged from the very decomposition into which he allows them just as continuously to slide.

The three people from whom I learned most about reading, and who seem to me exemplary in showing how reading asks for some of the same energies that go into writing, were not themselves writers of theory, and, so far as could be discerned, knew very little about Emerson, and still less about William James. They are G. Armour Craig, from whose teaching at Amherst I profited most as an undergraduate and who did nearly all of his critical work for and in his classes; F. R. Leavis, who was my tutor after that at Downing College, Cambridge, a famous classroom teacher who refused René Wellek's much publicized invitation to translate his practices into theoretical justifications; and Reuben Brower, from whom I never took a class but for whom I worked at Harvard from 1953 to 1961 in Hum 6.

I want to call attention to the importance of Brower's course and to give it a lineage. Out of several possibilities, the one I think most important belongs to a tradition of linguistic criticism that I have tried, ever since leaving the course, to locate in a line that runs from Emerson through William James, Kenneth Burke, Frost, Stein, and Stevens. As has been apparent, I read all of these as poets and read their poetry as a species of linguistic criticism, no less than are their lectures, letters, and essays. Together with the others in this line, they are at once grateful to the cultural inheritance of language and suspicious of it, congenitally uncertain as to the meaning of words and correspondingly attentive to nuance. Theirs is a criticism persuaded always of the instability of any formation of language.

Brower's course taught me, as did Emerson's linguistic skepticism, much that has since been theoretically formulated, though neither Brower, who boned up on Emerson for his Frost book, nor those in the course who subsequently were most responsive to European theory, ever knew enough about Emerson to acknowledge his influence on Hum 6. Surely Paul de Man did not, when, in the *TLS* of December 10, 1982, he wrote appreciatively that "my own awareness of the critical, even subversive, power of literary instruction does not stem from philosophical allegiances but from a very specific teaching experience." And then he identifies it: "In the 1950's . . . Reuben Brower . . . taught an undergraduate course [at Harvard] in General Education entitled 'The Interpretation of Literature' (better known on the Harvard campus and in the profession at large as Hum 6)."

Over nearly the same number of years, de Man and I were among the half-dozen or so section leaders in the course. Not all of them would find the word "subversive" appropriate to the kinds of activity with language that went on in class and that was asked for in the writing assignments out of class. It was my impression that only some of the teachers and still fewer of the students in the course were aware that their activity could prove to be subversive. Many thought of Hum 6 as a more subtle and ideologically neutral version of New Criticism, a mode of criticism which in my view, and for reasons I will get to presently, was in fact subservient to quite specific social and even religious forms of authority. It is therefore disappointing to discover that on other occasions de Man casually, or possibly for professionalist reasons, makes equations among New Criticism, close reading, Derrida, and himself, to the point where he gives the unintended and erroneous impression that any kind of critical-linguistic study which focuses on texts is by nature subversive. The spirit of Hum 6 and of its American derivations does seem to me "subversive," but only in quite limited ways.

It is in the very nature of Hum 6 that it has never blown its own horn. There was nothing of the theorist in Brower, and it could be argued, as did Robert Elliott in a commemoratory talk at the Modern Language Association meeting of 1976, that Brower in his writing might now and then have profitably been more of a theorist, especially when it came to the key term in his *Alexander Pope: The Poetry of Allusion*. Even more than his friend Leavis, he was disinclined to summarize what he was doing, and he avoided critical controversy as assiduously as Leavis sought it out. (The fourteen essays by people who had taught the course, edited by Brower and me and published in 1962 under the title *In Defense of Reading*,[2] is filled with good moments, but not one of the essays is polemical even to the point of contrasting the sort of thing we did in class with what went on in most other humanities and literature classes.) Given the degree to which the course anticipated and indeed moved beyond many later theoretical propositions about language, it is not surprising that those who taught it have not subsequently waxed theoretical about things they long ago took for granted. Of those who have since become known for their work in the academy, some, like Paul Bertram, Thomas Edwards, Neil Rudenstine, and William Pritchard, are indifferent when not opposed to out-and-out theorizing; others, like Paul Alpers, David Kalstone, Anne Ferry, and Margery Sabin have been hospitable to theoretical formulations of what they would be doing anyway; and those who have become known as theorists, like Neil Hertz, Peter Brooks, and de Man, readily admit some prior obligation to Hum 6.

In trying to understand where a course like Hum 6 came from, it is essential to remember that while the course itself flourished at Harvard in the mid-fifties and early sixties, which is when de Man got to know about its "subversiveness," a precursor had existed in a course which Armour Craig, Theodore Baird, and Brower had created at Amherst College in the preceding decade. The Amherst course was for sophomores, most of whom would have taken in their first year another course, specifically in writing, that was fashioned by Baird on lines that, despite his disclaimers, have been identified as Wittgensteinian. This freshman course was an even more radical immersion in the waywardness of language, too offbeat and subtle to be summarized here. English 19–20, as the sophomore course was called, appeared to be less daring than the Baird course, English 1–2, perhaps because it emphasized, as did courses then being given at other places, the close reading of texts or, in Brower's better phrase, "reading in slow motion."[3] For him reading ideally remained *in* motion, not choosing to encapsulate itself, as New Critical readings nearly always ultimately aspire to do. It was different from Brooks and Warren, with their *Understanding Poetry*—importantly so.

The Harvard undergraduates in Hum 6 numbered just over two hundred; they met together once a week for a lecture and then met again with section teachers in groups of about twenty-five. The sections were devoted to demonstrations, taking off from the lectures, and to discussions of the three-to-five-page papers written outside class every couple of weeks. These would be returned to the students heavily marked up, usually with complaints that something had not been shown sufficiently to derive from the language of the work in question. The introductory lectures at the beginning of each term—in the first term on reading a poem or story, in the second on reading a work within the context of other writings—were almost always given by Brower. Once past the first year of the course, which began in 1954, he now and again turned some of the lectures over to me, and after they joined the staff in 1956–57, to Ferry or de Man. The three of us ran the course whenever Brower was on leave, except on one such occasion when it was supervised by Craig, on a year's visit from Amherst. Ferry, de Man, and I were a bit older than the others on the staff; we had all taught elsewhere and had a fairly clear idea of what we wanted to do as critics. But we all shared with the rest of the group both a temperamental commitment to the course and an affectionate admiration for Brower as our leader and example. The teachers in Hum 6 were thought to have a special bond that set them off from other graduate students or junior faculty in literature at Harvard; many in the English department resented the course. Understandably so, since we taught students to respond to those inflections of language which most teachers of literature, even as they dig away at metaphoric patterns, often cannot hear or which they ignore in the interest of a variously motivated eloquence.

By describing our allegiance as "temperamental," I mean that we were willing, indeed anxious to deny ourselves the embarrassing Big Talk promised by the titles of the other Humanities courses, like "Ideas of Good and Evil" or "The Individual and Society." I think one reason why certain students became deeply attached to Hum 6 and have remained so for life is that it offered them a way to avoid such resounding terms. They discovered that *not* to become grand is often the best way to stay in a particularly vital relation to what you are reading. To Brower's recurrent question, "What is it like to read this?" they came upon an Emersonian answer without knowing Emerson—"An imaginative book," he says in "The Poet," "renders us much more service, at first, by stimulating us through its tropes, than afterward, when we arrive at the precise sense of the author." Emerson himself at other points makes the few exceptions to this proposal that need to be made. If the stimulation is "first," why should it not also be last? Why, in that case, should anyone want ever to arrive at a "precise sense"? Much better to practice the art of *not* arriving. We shared with Brower a wariness of the rhetorical power of the very things we taught—it could often be found to undo itself anyway—and we tried not to let it empower any rhetorical displays of our own. Like Craig, Brower seldom italicized anything he said when he addressed a work in class; he gave almost no indication that he was especially moved by a passage. Students, many of them not yet emotionally and certainly not intellectually formed, were grateful to discover that they were not to be emotionally or intellectually overawed by us or by the reading. They had simply to work on it, "concentrating," as de Man describes it, "on the way the meaning is conveyed rather than on meaning itself."

Deprived of illusions about "meaning," there was little chance that the students would become disillusioned about literature, as so many now claim to be, because it failed to measure up to a priori political or ideological purposes, including the ideologies of selfhood. Speaking with almost no heightening of voice, patiently inquiring, as the students were themselves asked to do, into the many possible and competing voices to be heard in writing, with all its waverings and fractures, Brower induced a feeling, without ever being explicit about it, that the human presence in any gathering of words was always elusive, existing as it did in the very tentative, sometimes self-doubting plays of sound.

We found it convenient to use canonical texts for what seem to me obvious reasons: first, because of the concentrated uses of language normally found in them and, second, because there is no better way to show that the grand cognitive achievements claimed for these same canonical works in other literature courses simply are not there. But a lot of time was also given to writings of no clear literary status, like samples of conversation, mottoes and aphorisms, or historical writings, as when the historian William Taylor, author of *Cavalier and Yankee* and a devoted member of the staff who had taught the earlier course at Amherst, led us through Parkman's *La Salle and the Discovery of the Great West*. We read letters, fragments from Simon Suggs (to complement *Adventures of Huckleberry Finn*), St. Thomas Aquinas (for his possible relevance to Joyce's *A Portrait of the Artist*), and writings by authors as marginal to the then-established canon as Edwin Muir and Sarah Orne Jewett. In choosing works for the introductory lectures and exercises, Brower preferred selections, like sketches from Jewett's *The Country of the Pointed Firs,* that discouraged any kind of magnification, or pieces that failed of the kinds of coherence most teachers look for. One year he began the course with an exercise on a short poem by Edwin Muir which, as an exasperated newcomer to the staff complained, simply "doesn't come together." This only confirmed the wisdom of the choice for Brower, who said simply, "Well, let's see what they can do with it." "Do with it," not "get out of it." The question he liked to ask on this and other occasions was, again, simply "What is it like to read this poem?"—the very hardest of questions, and not one likely to encourage a search for coherent patterns.

Any kind of close reading in the fifties and sixties came to be called New Criticism, no matter how different was Blackmur from Richards, or Empson from Leavis, or Burke from Tate; literary-critical histories of the period have still not made the requisite distinctions, in part because they are concerned with what got into publication almost to the exclusion of what went on in the classrooms with teachers who published little or not at all. Because I had studied with Cleanth Brooks at Yale for a year after Amherst, had taught from Brooks and Warren's *Understanding Poetry* at Williams College for two years after that, and had spent a year around Leavis's *Scrutiny* (all this before Hum 6), the term New Criticism seemed to me then, as it does now, exasperatingly inexact. It needed and needs to be localized.

The term designated for me an ideological mutation of I. A. Richards that was occurring not at all in Hum 6, but rather to the south of it at Yale. It had emerged before that still further south, at Vanderbilt, home of the Fugitive group that included Robert Penn Warren, John Crowe Ransom, and Allen Tate, and in the *Southern Review,* published at Baton Rouge, Louisiana, from 1935 to 1942. The term New Criticism was Ransom's, from a title of his in 1941. There was a heady mixture in this New Criticism of science-bashing, of Christianity (Fall of Man variety), and a lot of covertly political emphasis on how a successful poem or story achieves a workable coherence and organicism that nicely holds together all the tensions within it. It was to be inferred, I came to suspect, that the virtues found in a good poem were to be found also in your ideal agrarian community. The New Criticism's self-appointed enemy was the rationality and abstraction of northern, big-city capitalism. T. S. Eliot's description of his train trip into the south from New England at the beginning of *After Strange Gods* —the lectures at the University of Virginia that became the 1934 book he apparently later wanted to forget (in part for its anti-Semitism)—is a good indication of his alliance with some of the cultural mythologies of New Criticism. Still another clue to this ideological affiliation exists in Eliot's essay of 1923 entitled *"Ulysses,* Order, and Myth." It is there that he talks about "the panorama of futility and anarchy which is contemporary history" and suggests that it can be given order—"order" was a New Critical buzzword—by the mythic method of Joyce's novel and, though he is too discreet to mention it, of another work of the same year, his own *The Waste Land.*

At Amherst, Eliot was never to be the dominant presence

he became at Yale during the ascendency there of its New Criticism—which helps explain why the negative assessments of Eliot from Harold Bloom (Yale Ph.D., 1955) are more emphatic than my own—or even at Harvard, where Matthiessen wrote his early and influential *The Achievement of T. S. Eliot.* When he found himself teaching *The Waste Land,* for example, Brower could never read aloud the ending, "Shanti   shanti   shanti," without showing evident distaste.

The Amherst people had a great poet-critic of their own, Robert Frost, and Frost was quite open, though the Amherst group has never sufficiently picked up on this, about his attachments to William James and Emerson. Frost was far too astute to box himself in by attacking Eliot head-on in public, and their final meetings in London in 1957 were affectionate and admiring. However, as I mentioned earlier, Eliot was the likely target of the urbanely disdainful remark in Frost's letter to *The Amherst Student* in 1935 that "Anyone who has achieved the least form to be sure of it, is lost to the larger excruciations." And Louis Untermeyer reports his saying in 1940 that "Eliot and I have our similarities and our differences. We are both poets and we both like to play. That's the similarity. The difference is this: I like to play euchre. He likes to play Eucharist." To put this somewhat differently, Frost never yearned for Eliot's "still point." He expected, again, no more than momentary stays against confusion; for him "confusion" resided not so much in "the futility and anarchy which is contemporary history" as in all of history at any time. "The background is hugeness and confusion," as he puts it in the *Amherst Student* letter, "shading away from where we stand into black and utter chaos; and against the background any small man-made figure of order and concentration." The "order" is manmade and temporary.

Eliot's exaltation of the so-called mythic method—along with Joyce's endorsements, however skittish, of charts of mythic and other correspondences for each of his chapters —can be shown to have had a profoundly damaging effect on the readings not only of *The Waste Land, Ulysses,* and other modernist works, but on the reading of literature in general. The damage is epitomized in such influential codifications as Joseph Frank's 1945 essay in *Sewanee Review* called "Spatial Form in Modern Literature," where it is proposed that Eliot, Pound, Proust, Joyce, and Djuna Barnes "ideally intend the reader to apprehend their work spatially, in a moment of time, rather than as a sequence." Readers have of course always done that to some extent with any text, and, to keep their sanity, people regularly do something like it to the events of their lives, reassembling them into what Barthes called "stenographic space." The *act* of reading, however, is not at all the same as remembering the text thereafter or reassembling it. It is an experience in time and not in space; we read, we know "what it is like to read," in sequence. Spatial reading represents an unfortunate triumph of the eye over the ear.

This distinction between eye and ear was especially important to Frost. As he admitted when writing to John Cournos in July 1914, he chose to "cultivate . . . the hearing imagination rather than the seeing imagination though I should not want to be without the latter." Earlier that same year he had written to another correspondent, John Bartlett, "The ear is the only true writer and the only true reader. I have known people who could read without hearing the sentence sounds and they were the fastest readers. Eye readers we call them. They get the meaning by glances. But they are bad readers because they miss the best part of what a good writer puts into his work." Beginning in 1916, when he first joined the Amherst faculty, and during yearly visits of some duration thereafter for most of his life, Frost was a seminal figure at Amherst, not only while Brower was teaching there but while Brower was himself a student. (He graduated summa cum laude in 1930.) Frost remembered hearing the undergraduate Brower read aloud an Elizabethan poem and saying on the spot, "I give you an A for life." "Goodness sake," he remarked, "the way his voice fell into those lines." Many of the Hum 6 staff had also been at Amherst while Frost was around, including me, William Taylor, Thomas Edwards, William Pritchard, and Neil Hertz. So were the poets David Ferry, Richard Wilbur, and James Merrill. Ferry wrote an undergraduate dissertation on Stevens in 1948, and Merrill a dissertation on Proust in 1947, both supervised by Brower.

What I take to be the strongest years of Amherst English were in the decade before Brower's departure for Harvard in 1953. The department then included, as I have mentioned, Armour Craig and Theodore Baird, who were as close to Frost as Brower was, Craig possibly more so. Craig's few published essays on nineteenth-century English fiction and his teaching of it anticipated by two decades the now-familiar critical focus on how precariously its structure sustains the moral and social rhetorics of judgment through to the crucial endings of works like *Vanity Fair* or *Dombey and Son* or *Middlemarch*. In 1966, what would now be called a deconstructive reading of *Adventures of Huckleberry Finn* in my *A World Elsewhere* illustrated the kind of thing Craig showed us how to do long before the term "deconstruction" was used to describe it. Craig was then and still is a devoted reader of Kenneth Burke, nearly as much as of Frost and, I assume, of Wittgenstein. (It is pertinent in that regard that James Guetti, yet another Amherst graduate, has recently been showing the importance of Wittgenstein to contemporary literary criticism.) As for Burke, Craig in the early fifties considered changing the vocabulary of English 19–20, which had derived from Richards as well as Frost, so as to feature Burke's pentad, in *A Grammar of Motives,* of "act," "scene," "agent," "agency," and "purpose."

The antipathy among Amherst people to any such proliferation of metalanguage fortunately prevailed, however. And even if the terminology had been adopted it would not have made the emphasis less Frostian, since Frost's insistence on the dramatic, on the drama of and among words, anticipates what Burke's was to be, even in detail. In a letter to L. W. Payne, Jr., in March 1936, Frost repeats his earlier claims that "I've just found out what makes a piece of writing good. . . . it is making the sentences talk to each other as two or more speakers do in drama." This presages Burke's repeated argument that a sentence may itself epitomize literature conceived as symbolic action. As he would have it, somebody is always doing something in a sentence to somebody else; that is, the grammatical elements "talk" to one another. Similarly, Burke's pentad has all the ingredients called for by Frost in his preface to *A Way Out* in 1929: "Everything written is as good as it is dramatic. It need not declare itself in form, but it is drama or it is nothing. By whom, where, and when is the question."

It is in line with this that Brower's lifelong regard for Leavis, whom he first met at Cambridge University in 1932, is best understood. Leavis was the brilliant champion in English criticism of the 1930s and 1940s of what he liked to call "the dramatic use of language." His repeated emphasis on that phrase has never, I think, been rightly understood. By "dramatic" he means to refer, as do Frost and Burke (whose term is "dramatistic") to the way words and sentences "talk to each other," the way they undo and reconstitute each other beyond the grasp of critical interpretations that look for unity and order. Ultimately, morality for Leavis had less to do with attitudes, though there is an excessive attitudinizing morality in him, than with the way one uses words. To focus in this manner on the dramatic is to look in writing for some active consent to a chastening fact: that words exist independently of the uses to which anyone, specifically including the reader, wants to put them. No matter how powerful the writer or the reader may be, his or her relation to words on a page is of necessity dialogic, a recognition that scarcely awaited the current Bakhtinian hoopla. The struggle for verbal consciousness must not be left out of art, as Lawrence said in 1920, and that includes the art of reading. Frost, Burke, and Leavis, all of them central to the kinds of reading asked for by Baird and Craig at Amherst and later by Brower and his staff at Harvard, share a conviction that, as Frost puts it in a letter in 1938 to R. P. T. Coffin, "poetry is the renewal of words forever and ever." That sentiment obviously informs the title of my own *The Renewal of Literature,* no less than its subtitle, *Emersonian Reflections.*

Emerson is a nourishing source for the kind of reading whose pedagogical career I have tried to describe, a claim that will disturb only the most benighted of Francophile theoreticians. Given that Brower was first of all a classicist, that de Man (though his translation of *Moby-Dick* into Flemish appeared in 1945) knew essentially nothing about American literature, and that Wittgenstein and Leavis, who were friends of a sort in Cambridge in the early 1930s, have been brought into these equations, I cannot be supposed to think that Emersonian "reflections" occur only in Concord, Massachusetts. Among the many indications that Emerson did not regard himself or his country as specific to time and place is the remark in his Journals for March-April 1847 that "A good scholar will find Aristophanes & Hafiz & Rabelais full of American history." It can as aptly be said that a good scholar will find Emerson full of de Man, Derrida, and Barthes, just as, quite differently, he is full of Frost and Burke.

The most vital of these differences has to do with the vexed question of self-presence in writing and reading. For Emerson, writing and reading do not, merely because of the deconstructive tendencies inherent in language, dissolve human presence; human presence comes into existence *in* writing and reading thanks to these traceable actions by which, through troping, deconstructive tendencies are acknowledged and contravened. There exists a crude and over-emphatic perception of the assumed antagonism between deconstruction in language, on the one hand, and, on the other, the possible shaping, in language, of Emersonian selves. After all, why do words even need to be renewed, as Emerson insists they do, if not in recognition of their deconstructive potential? How, indeed, can something so problematic and fragile as Emersonian self-presence be understood except in the context of its opposite—the self-abandonment which for him is the only sure antidote to conformity, including conformity to one's own rhetoric?

In calling attention to Brower's vocal unassertiveness—as if he were heeding Emerson's warnings in "Self-Reliance"—and to the low-keyed precision of the readings he offered in class and in his writing, I want to suggest a consonance between this way of reading literary works and the kind of elusive self-presence that is to be found in them if we but listen for inflections of sound. A word so big and, by now, so prejudicial as "phonocentrism" grotesquely magnifies the true image of voice in writing; voice just as often is trying to marginalize itself, to evade those invitations to self-assertion that exist all around it in literary and social blandishments. To expect that the self in literature is an entity or a center is as credulous as to expect to find an actual pole when you get to the northern and southern extremities of the world. The poles are long since fallen, including, as Cleopatra and Shakespeare know, the soldier's pole.

My own rhetoric about absent or fallen poles raises once again the question of whether the word "subversive" is appropriate to Hum 6. The term has perhaps become too grandiose for the course I have been describing; the Glendowers of literary theory are forever using it, as if at its mention "the frame and huge foundation of the earth / Shaked like a coward." Meanwhile, the people I have associated with this course, from the Hum 6 staff all the way back to Emerson, harbored no such illusions as are now abroad about the power of reading or of writing, especially in criticism. Reading and writing are activities which for them require endless scruple. That is how the activity of reading begins, how it is carried on, and why, so long as the words are in front of you, it should never end. It need never be broken off out of some guilty feeling that the activity of reading is not sufficiently political or socially beneficial. It is to be understood as a lonely discipline that makes no great claims for itself. Reading conducted under such a regimen can be subversive only to the extent that it encourages us to get under and turn over not systems and institutions, but only words. The words most susceptible to subversion tend to be found in the works called literature because in literature they are quite consciously meant to be susceptible. And yet any words can be gotten under and turned over, including those in philosophical works and in all kinds of social and political writing. As we congratulate ourselves on subversive readings of nonliterary language, however, it should be kept in mind that the talent for such reading is often acquired by work done with literature itself, even while it is literature that is nowadays frequently under attack as being in league with some of the least commendable of our social arrangements. Criticism should remember Emerson's admonition in "The Conservative"—"The past has baked your loaf, and in the strengths of its bread you would break up the oven"—and begin to calm down.

NOTES

Introduction

1. The statements about James's pragmatism made by Peirce in *The Monist*, 15 (1905) and in the letter to Mrs. Ladd-Franklin are cited in Ralph Barton Perry, *The Thought and Character of William James* (Boston: Little, Brown, 1935), 1:535.

2. Chapman's essay on Emerson can be found in *The Selected Writings of John Jay Chapman*, ed. Jacques Barzun (New York: Farrar, Straus, and Cudahy, 1957), 150–202.

3. For some crisp and informative comments on the adulation of Emerson and the exceptions taken to it by D. H. Lawrence, T. S. Eliot, and others, see the introductory section called "Hagiography" in Joel Porte, *Representative Man: Ralph Waldo Emerson in His Time* (New York: Oxford University Press, 1979), 3–9.

4. All references to Emerson's Journals, unless otherwise indicated, are to Joel Porte, ed., *Emerson in His Journals* (Cambridge: Harvard University Press, 1982).

5. Cavell writes, "Working within an aspiration of philosophy that feeds, and is fed by, a desire to inherit Emerson and Thoreau as thinkers, I take it for granted that their thinking is unknown to the culture whose thinking they worked to found (I mean culturally unpossessed, unassumable among those who care for books, however possessed by shifting bands of individuals), in a way it would not be thinkable for Kant and Schiller and Goethe to be unknown to the culture of Germany, or Descartes and Rousseau to France, or Locke and Hume and John Stuart Mill to England." See Stanley Cavell, "Emer-

son, Coleridge, Kant," *In Quest of the Ordinary* (Chicago: University of Chicago Press, 1988), 27.

6. "Writing Off the Self" is the final chapter of *The Renewal of Literature* (New York: Random House, 1987), 182–223.

7. A powerful critique of this illusion can be found throughout Leo Bersani's *The Culture of Redemption* (Cambridge: Harvard University Press, 1990). See also the "Prologue" in *The Renewal of Literature,* 3–66.

8. Stein's *The Geographical History of America, or the Relation of Human Nature to the Human Mind* is extremely hard to come by, even in university libraries; this passage can be found in an edition, with an introduction by Thornton Wilder, published in 1936 by Random House, pp. 179–180.

9. This and all subsequent quotations from Emerson's essays are taken from Joel Porte, ed., *Ralph Waldo Emerson: Essays and Lectures* (New York: The Library of America, 1983).

10. The distinction between texts and works is also drawn, in a way that faults the many distinguished contemporary critics who ignore it, in a review article by Tanselle entitled "Textual Criticism and Deconstruction," *Studies in Bibliography,* 43 (1990), 1–33. He there points to some of the consequences in criticism and theory of the now inveterate habit of using the word "texts" to mean "works," and his examples are the essays contributed to the volume under review—*Deconstruction and Criticism* (New York: Continuum, 1979)—by Geoffrey Hartman, Harold Bloom, Paul de Man, Jacques Derrida, and J. Hillis Miller.

11. Cited in Gregory Jay, *T. S. Eliot and the Poetics of Literary History* (Baton Rouge: Louisiana State University Press, 1983), 17. A few pages earlier, Jay makes an essential point about Emerson—that his "self-reliance depends upon identification, or a speculative relationship, with the inherited function of the father as self-begetter" (p. 15).

12. This and the next paragraph are taken with very little revision from my introduction to the 1990 Oxford University Press selected edition of the essays and poems of Emerson, p. xix.

13. A complex reading adequate to Emerson's idea of "individualism" has been called for by his best interpreters as far back as Santayana in 1903, but the concept still fails to be generally accepted or understood. George Kateb is admirably lucid on the subject: "The nobility of the Emersonian aspiration lies in transcending the ideal of individualism understood as the cultivation and expression of personality, precisely because Emerson, like his great colleagues Thoreau and Whitman, knows how social, and not individualistic, such an ideal is." George Kateb, "Individualism, Communitarianism, and Docility," *Social Research,* 56:4 (1989), 938. Santayana's essay remains one of the very best on Emerson, in part for his arguing that "Potentiality, cosmic liberty, nature perpetually transforming and recovering her energy, formed his loftiest theme; but the sense of riddance in escaping kings, churches, cities, and eventually self and even humanity, was the nearer and if possible the livelier emotion." Santayana's essay, "Emerson's Poems Proclaim the Divinity of Nature, with Freedom as His Profoundest Ideal," was given as an address during Emerson Memorial Week at Harvard College in May 1903. It is reprinted in *George Santayana's America,* collected with an introduction by James Ballowe (Urbana: University of Illinois Press, 1967), 84–96. The quoted passage is on p. 91.

I. Superfluous Emerson

1. Richard Grusin discusses the idea of the "superfluous" in relation to Thoreau in an as yet unpublished essay entitled "Thoreau, Extravagance, and the Economy of Nature." See also his " 'Put God in Your Debt': Emerson's Economy of Expenditure," *PMLA,* 103:1 (1988), 33–44.
2. There is a good account of James's despondencies during the 1860s and into the 1870s in Howard M. Feinstein, *Becoming William James* (Ithaca: Cornell University Press, 1984).
3. See William Keach, *Shelley's Style* (New York: Methuen, 1984), especially the chapter entitled "Shelley's Speed," 154–183.

4. The passage from "Lecture on the Times," as it appears in the Library of America edition of *Ralph Waldo Emerson: Essays and Lectures,* is as follows: "What we are? and Whither we tend? We do not wish to be deceived. Here we drift, like white sail across the wild ocean, now bright on the wave, now darkling in the trough of the sea;—but from what port did we sail? Who knows? Or to what port are we bound? Who knows? There is no one to tell us but such poor weather-tossed mariners as ourselves, whom we speak as we pass, or who have hoisted some signal, or floated to us some letter in a bottle from far. But what know they more than we? They also found themselves on this wondrous sea" (168).

5. At the beginning of the concluding section of the essay, Emerson writes: "Illusion, Temperament, Succession, Surface, Surprise, Reality, Subjectiveness—these are threads on the loom of time, these are the lords of life." Each of these "lords of life" is apparently meant to correspond to one of the seven preceding sections of the essay; but while these sections are set off from each other by spacing, none carries any such printed title. A helpful account of these itemizations of the essay's subjects, along with some reservations as to their usefulness, can be found in Sharon Cameron, "Representing Grief: Emerson's 'Experience,' " *Representations,* 15 (1986), 21.

6. In an exploration of the sentence "Nothing is left us now but death," Stanley Cavell develops an argument similar to mine about the relation of Waldo's death to Emerson's writing—to the actual accomplishments *in* the writing, word by word, of the essay. Stanley Cavell, *This New Yet Unapproachable America* (Albuquerque: Living Batch Press, 1989), 106–107.

7. Pertinent discussion of Emerson's shifting attitudes toward the market economy can be found in Michael T. Gilmore, *American Romanticism and the Marketplace* (Chicago: University of Chicago Press, 1985), especially chap. 1, "Emerson and the Persistence of Commodity," 18–34; Richard Grusin, "Put God in Your Debt"; and Howard Horwitz, "The Standard Oil Trust as Emersonian Hero," *Raritan Quarterly,* 6:4 (1987), 97–119.

8. As George Kateb has brilliantly suggested, "modesty" can pose its own sort of threat to individualism and to such freedom as individual expression needs for itself within any democratic grouping. Speaking of Tocqueville's analysis of individualism, as against Foucault's, he refers to "the intimidating pressure of modesty, which the individual feels in the face of all the others, his equals, and which, by issuing in private retreat and self-absorption, causes an expansion of the tutelary activism of state power." George Kateb, "Individualism, Communitarianism, and Docility," 934.

9. Some interpretations that touch effectively on this aspect of *Moby-Dick* are by Wai-chee Dimock, *Empire for Liberty: Melville and the Poetics of Individualism* (Princeton: Princeton University Press, 1989); C. L. R. James, *Mariners, Renegades and Castaways* (London: Allison & Bushby, 1985); and Donald Pease in the remarkable final chapter of his *Visionary Compacts: American Renaissance Writings in Cultural Context* (Madison: University of Wisconsin Press, 1987), 235–275.

10. James Cox observed some time ago, in a seminal essay on Emerson, that "Getting out of the 'I,' the personal pronoun, and over the deaths of loved ones is no tired or traditional 'spiritual' vision for Emerson precisely because it is a literal breathing in, or inspiration, of the death of life." James Cox, "R. W. Emerson: The Circles of the Eye," in *Emerson: Prophecy, Metamorphosis, and Influence,* ed. David Levin (New York: Columbia University Press, 1975), 72. See also one of the very best of recent books on Emerson, B. L. Packer, *Emerson's Fall: A New Interpretation of the Major Essays* (New York: Continuum, 1982), 50–54.

11. In "Experience," Emerson could be said to eradicate the role of Lidian, and therefore of women more generally, in the process of usurping all parental authority for creation. According to Mark Edmundson in *Towards Reading Freud,* a work that has many brilliant pages on Emerson, this project of erasure is summarized and enacted by Freud in his invention of the Oedipal myth. "For if there is a significant place for femininity in Freud's Oedipal myth," he writes, "it is only

at the source, or oracle; in constructing his own genealogy, in which he plays the part of the enlightened descendent of Sophocles and Shakespeare, Freud erases the role of the woman. He is the culmination of an all-male line: no female presence qualifies or calls into doubt the purity of his symbolic lineage." Mark Edmundson, *Towards Reading Freud: Self-Creation in Milton, Wordsworth, Emerson, and Sigmund Freud* (Princeton: Princeton University Press, 1990), 40.

12. An account of this episode is given in the volume of Leon Edel's biography entitled *Henry James: The Conquest of London 1870–1881* (Philadelphia: Lippincott, 1963), 414.

13. Sharon Cameron is notably acute in her reading of this passage: "Emerson brings together the loss of the child and the loss of the estate, then, to preserve on one level a crucial disparity between the feeling and the words which degrade it that has crucially been violated on another—the disparity between a trivial and a consequential loss." Cameron, "Representing Grief," 22.

14. See Peter Ackroyd, *T. S. Eliot: A Life* (London: Hamish Hamilton, 1984), 40–41.

15. George Kateb, "Thinking of Human Extinction (II): Emerson and Whitman," *Raritan Quarterly,* 6:3 (1987), 18–19.

16. Charles S. Peirce, *Selected Writings of Charles S. Peirce,* ed. Philip P. Wiener (New York: Dover Publications, 1958), 383.

II. The Transfiguration of Work

1. Cynthia Griffin Wolff offers the best discussion I have seen of "Essential Oils." Cynthia Griffin Wolff, *Emily Dickinson* (New York: Knopf, 1986), 216–217. She argues that Emerson's influence on Dickinson was limited, pp. 141–142. For perceptive commentary on the literary relations between Emerson and Dickinson, see also Evan Carton, *The Rhetoric of American Romance* (Baltimore: Johns Hopkins University Press, 1985) 28–30, 42–45, 129–130.

2. I offer a roughly similar interpretation of "Upon Appleton

House" in *The Performing Self* (New York: Oxford University Press, 1971), 95–98.

3. Frost's most fully articulated discussions of "the sound of sense" and "sentence sounds" occur in several letters written to various correspondents in 1913 and 1914; they can be found indexed under these topic headings in *Selected Letters of Robert Frost*, ed. Lawrance Thompson (New York: Holt, Rinehart and Winston, 1964).

4. Henry James, Sr.'s remark is quoted in John McAleer, *Ralph Waldo Emerson: Days of Encounter* (Boston: Little, Brown, 1984), 387.

5. Ralph Barton Perry, *The Thought and Character of William James* (Boston: Little, Brown, 1935), 2:68.

6. See Constance Webb, *Richard Wright: A Biography* (New York: Putnam, 1988), 249.

7. George Kateb, "Individualism, Communitarianism, and Docility," 926. Cavell expresses similar reservations about Dewey, as compared to Emerson, when he remarks that "For Emerson, as for Kant, putting the philosophical intellect into practice remains a question for philosophy. For a thinker such as John Dewey it becomes, as I might put it, merely a problem. That is, Dewey assumes that science shows what intelligence is and that what intelligent practice is pretty much follows from that; the mission of philosophy is to get the Enlightenment to happen. For Emerson the mission is rather, or as much, to awaken us to why it is happening as it is, negatively not affirmatively." Stanley Cavell, *This New Yet Unapproachable America*, 95.

8. Frank Lentricchia makes a similar point: "Though not practice for its own sake, pragmatism cannot say what practice should be aimed at without ceasing to be pragmatism, without violating its reverence for experimental method. . . . Pragmatism's best insight, that knowledge is an instrument for doing work in this world, cannot help us to do the social work of transformation implied in the Deweyan slogan 'society as a function of education.' " Frank Lentricchia, *Criticism and Social Change* (Chicago: University of Chicago Press, 1983), 4.

9. "Symbolic action" is a persistent theme in all of Burke's criticism, especially in the essays in *Language as Symbolic Action* (Berkeley: University of California Press, 1966).

10. Similarities between Eliot's views of the relation between art and emotion and the views expressed by Clive Bell and Dora Marsden are mentioned in Louis Menand's indispensible *Discovering Modernism* (New York: Oxford University Press, 1987), 142.

11. Bloom would agree, especially of Emerson and Stein, that the American writers I am discussing do not easily reveal any "anxiety of influence," but he still insists, as I would not, on the determining if repressed evidences of anxiety. Thus, writing of the passage from *The Geographical History of America* which I discuss in the Introduction, he locates in it "a ruthless strategy for subverting any author's sense of belatedness, of coming after Shakespeare." See his introduction to *Gertrude Stein* (Modern Critical Views Series), ed. Harold Bloom (New York: Chelsea House, 1990), 2.

12. See my *The Renewal of Literature* (New York: Random House, 1987), 178–180; also, "The Voicing of Things," a new afterword to *Robert Frost: The Work of Knowing*, reissued in 1990 by Stanford University Press, pp. 315–338. For an extended analysis of "Never Again Would Birds' Song Be the Same," especially with reference to signs and tracings, see my "Robert Frost," in *Voices and Visions: The Poet in America*, ed. Helen Vendler (New York: Random House, 1987), 91–121.

13. I am referring to the essays in Eric Hobsbawm and Terence Ranger, eds., *The Invention of Tradition* (Cambridge: Cambridge University Press, 1984), especially Hobsbawm's introduction, "Inventing Traditions," pp. 1–14.

14. Of these sentences, Dewey observes: "When Emerson, speaking of the chronology of history, designated the There and Then as 'wild, savage, and preposterous,' he also drew the line which marks him off from transcendentalism—which is the idealism of a Class. In sorry truth, the idealist has too

frequently conspired with the sensualist to deprive the pressing and so the passing Now of value which is spiritual. Through the joint work of such malign conspiracy, the common man is not, or at least does not know himself for, an idealist." John Dewey, "Ralph Waldo Emerson," in John Dewey and Joseph Ratner, eds., *Characters and Events* (New York: Henry Holt, 1929), 1:75.

15. Commenting on Van Wyck Brooks's *America's Coming of Age,* David Bromwich takes note of the fact that Brooks "understood pragmatism as a decadent idealism that had betrayed genius in the name of practical power." I share Bromwich's uneasiness about Brooks's position and agree that it ignores an Emersonian pragmatist support for revolt that is so expansive in its expression, especially in Emerson, as to be unadaptable to any very particular design for change, particularly when change is confused with the attainment of material success. But it is obvious that for me the rhetoric of Emerson, and especially of James and Dewey, does lend itself to Brooks's interpretation, no less than to those vulgar adaptations of pragmatism which Brooks tends to confuse with the whole of it. See David Bromwich, *A Choice of Inheritance: Self and Community from Edmund Burke to Robert Frost* (Cambridge: Harvard University Press, 1989) 153–155. See also the illuminating discussions of some of these matters in Olaf Hansen, *Aesthetic Individualism and Practical Intellect* (Princeton: Princeton University Press, 1990).

16. Jacques Barzun has described the "poeticizing of war" as a general phenomenon in the West during the period 1870–1914, especially in *fin de siècle* Europe. Jacques Barzun, *Darwin, Marx, Wagner: Critique of a Heritage* (Chicago: University of Chicago Press, 1941), 90ff. See also Daniel Aaron, *The Unwritten War: American Writers and the Civil War* (New York: Oxford University Press, 1975), where he observes (pp. 37–38) that "Emerson worked out his dialectics of war and peace, and had no difficulty accommodating it to American facts" well before the Civil War began. An exceptionally well-

documented account of these developments is given by Michael Lopez, "Emerson's Rhetoric of War," in *Prospects: An Annual of American Cultural Studies,* ed. Jack Salzman (New York: Cambridge University Press, 1987), 293–320.

17. Dewey's letter to Klyce is quoted in Gerald Myers, *William James: His Life and Thought* (New Haven: Yale University Press, 1986), 602.

18. Michael Lopez relates Emerson's occasional exaltations of war to his repeated expressions of antagonism to any fixed idea of the self. There are similar suggestions throughout Julie Ellison's *Emerson's Romantic Style* (Princeton: Princeton University Press, 1984). See Michael Lopez, "Transcendental Failure: 'The Palace of Spiritual Power,' " in Joel Porte, ed., *Emerson: Prospect and Retrospect* (Cambridge: Harvard University Press, 1982), 40. See also Stephen Donadio, "Emerson, Christian Identity, and the Dissolution of the Social Order," in Quentin Anderson, Stephen Donadio, and Steven Marcus, eds., *Art, Politics, and Will: Essays in Honor of Lionel Trilling* (New York: Basic Books, 1977), 120–121. It needs to be kept in mind, however, that the "self" in Emerson, *as* we read his prose, never is obliterated or extinguished; rather, it is often the case that any version of it immediately being made present in the writing is also being phased out in the verbal process by which a new version of the "self" is emerging.

19. Some time after writing this sentence, I found the point of it confirmed in the *London Review of Books* (25 July 1991) where, in an essay on Dewey as intellectual hero, Richard Rorty remarks that "the Cold War was a good war." It is left at that, no explanations needed. I suppose he calls the Cold War good because it was James's moral equivalent of a hot war, without bloodletting, that is, on a global scale at least; or "good" because it brought to conclusion Dewey's own lifelong effort to expose the bankruptcy of Communism. But in a sense I take to be more crucially pragmatic, it cannot be called good. The Cold War was conducted on the domestic front in a manner that has done unacceptable damage to the

victor country's sense of itself and of its relations to other nations and other people. The rhetoric and habits of mind inculcated over its long duration have by now made the pursuit of truth in American public life close to impossible, perpetuating, under the cover of national security, the mythology of the United States as an immaculate conception and, with that, making a virtue of ignorance and dismissiveness when it comes to those others, including dissenting and marginalized fellow citizens, who do not subscribe to the myth or who find themselves in conditions of life that belie it.

20. In one of his many fine essays on Santayana, Henry Samuel Levinson observes that "Santayana used an aesthetic language of spirit to break away from American spiritual exceptionalism altogether. He participated neither in the tradition of the American Jeremiad nor, for that matter, in the tradition of American anti-Jeremiad. He found rhetorically attractive ways to present America neither as the be-all and end-all of spirit nor as exceptionally antispiritual. America had its spiritual promises and problems, on the view he developed, but they were not intrinsically greater or smaller than any of the other nations of the world." Henry Samuel Levinson, "Santayana's Contribution to American Religious Philosophy," *Journal of the American Academy of Religion,* 52:1 (1984), 54.

21. A similar linkage of poets and soldiers has been noticed in Emerson by David Porter, *Emerson and Literary Change* (Cambridge: Harvard University Press, 1978), 107.

III. The Reinstatement of the Vague

1. See the discussion of Edwards and language in Perry Miller, *Errand into the Wilderness* (Cambridge: Harvard University Press, 1956), 177–183.

2. Some of the resemblances between Paterian and Emersonian pragmatist aesthetics are explored in my "Pater, Joyce, Eliot," *James Joyce Quarterly* 26:1 (1988), 21–35.

3. The influence of William James on Stein, and specifically on "Melanctha," is extensively discussed in Lisa Ruddick, *Reading Gertrude Stein: Body, Text, Gnosis* (Ithaca: Cornell University Press, 1990). See especially the sections entitled " 'Melanctha' and the Psychology of William James," pp. 13–25 and "The Style of 'Melanctha': Stein's Resistance to James," pp. 33–41. In her valuable study of Stein, Harriet Chessman discovers the influence of Emerson in "Melanctha" as well as of James. Harriet Scott Chessman, *The Public Is Invited to Dance* (Stanford: Stanford University Press, 1989), 41–53, 156–161. See also Steven Myer, "Stein and Emerson," *Raritan Quarterly*, 10:2 (1990), 87–115.

4. In an essay on the *Federalist* papers, John Burt makes the point that the founding of the Republic depended, to some measure, on a tacit agreement not to clarify differences or divergent interests, but to resort to phrasings vague enough that contending parties, even in future disputes not then predictable, could depend on enough flexibility in constitutional and legislative language to accommodate opposing interests. See John Burt, "Tyranny and the Public Sphere in *The Federalist*," *Raritan Quarterly*, forthcoming.

5. In particular, see the discussions of "crossing" in what Bloom calls a "crisis poem," in his *Wallace Stevens: The Poems of Our Climate* (Ithaca: Cornell University Press, 1976), 2.

6. See the informative reference to this passage in Catharine Stimpson's *Where the Meanings Are: Feminism and Cultural Spaces* (New York: Methuen, 1988), 117–118. Stimpson points out that Stein's note after the passage—"Not as if it was tried"—has at least two meanings: "no one has really done this before; if you are going to do this, do it as if no one really had before; i.e., begin again." The passage from *Patriarchal Poetry* can be found in *The Yale Gertrude Stein*, ed. Richard Kostelanetz (New Haven: Yale University Press, 1980), 111.

7. Apropos the implications in Stevens of the phrase "as if," see Helen Vendler's essay "The Qualified Assertions of Wallace Stevens," in *The Act of Mind*, ed. Roy Harvey Pearce and

J. Hillis Miller (Baltimore: Johns Hopkins University Press, 1965), 163–178.

8. The word "éclat" is used with negative connotations in a letter to him in 1822, a year after his graduation from Harvard, written by his aunt, Mary Moody Emerson (he liked to call her "Father Mum"). Replying to his complaint that he had been having difficulty with his writing, she remarked that "there is a time approaching that I dread worse than this sweet stagnation, when your muse shall be dragged into éclat." Mary Moody Emerson's use of the term was pointed out to me by Joe Thomas, and can be found in George Tolman, *Mary Moody Emerson*, p. 21. This monograph, a 1902 address by Tolman to the Concord Antiquarian Society, was privately printed in 1929.

9. Matthew Lewis, while a student in a seminar of mine at Rutgers, discovered some correspondences between this first section of "The Rock" and a passage in James's *The Will to Believe*. The echoes are so striking—as are the echoes in James of Emerson's "rock" in "Experience"—that I quote in full the two paragraphs. They are from the chapter called "The Moral Philosopher and the Moral Life" in *The Will to Believe* (Cambridge: Harvard University Press, 1979), 150: "Were all other things, gods and men and starry heavens, blotted out from this universe, and were there left but one rock with two loving souls upon it, that rock would have as thoroughly moral a constitution as any possible world which the eternities and immensities could harbor. It would be a tragic constitution, because the rock's inhabitants would die. But while they lived, there would be real good things and real bad things in the universe; there would be obligations, claims, and expectations; obediences, refusals, and disappointments; compunctions and longings for harmony to come again, and inward peace of conscience when it was restored; there would, in short, be a moral life, whose active energy would have no limit but the intensity of interest in each other with which the hero and heroine might be endowed.

"We, on this terrestrial globe, so far as the visible facts go, are just like the inhabitants of such a rock. Whether a God exist, or whether no God exist, in yon blue heaven above us bent, we form at any rate an ethical republic here below. And the first reflection which this leads to is that ethics have as genuine and real a foothold in a universe where the highest consciousness is human, as in a universe where there is a God as well. 'The religion of humanity' affords a basis for ethics as well as theism does. Whether the purely human system can gratify the philosopher's demand as well as the other is a different question, which we ourselves must answer ere we close."

10. J. Hillis Miller, *The Linguistic Moment* (Princeton University Press, 1985), 394.

11. Though he has a somewhat different target in mind, Edward Said voices an objection similar to mine against what he calls "these tremendous conflations, inflations, exaggerations" that can occur in the practice of criticism. His 1989 Wellek Lectures in Critical Theory, delivered at the University of California at Irvine, offer some brilliant dissections of the processes by which the artistic productions of particular groups and of particular historical moments are made to seem universally applicable to all times, persons, and cultures. The lectures were published as *Musical Elaborations* (Columbia University Press, 1991). See p. 52 and all of chap. 2, "On the Transgressive Elements in Music," pp. 34–72. See also in this regard Eric Hobsbawm and Terence Ranger, eds., *The Invention of Tradition,* and specifically Hobsbawm's "Introduction: Inventing Tradition."

IV. Reading Pragmatically

1. Kermode's brilliantly argued and persuasive discussions of the so-called canon are to be found most readily in his *History and Value* (Oxford: Clarendon Press, 1988), 108–127 and in *An*

Appetite for Poetry (Cambridge: Harvard University Press, 1989), 189–207.

2. *In Defense of Reading* was published in 1962 (New York: Dutton), and obviously only those who had taught the course before that date were asked to contribute. The contributors, in order of appearance on the title page, were: Reuben A. Brower, Paul de Man, William H. Pritchard, Neil Hertz, Anne Davidson Ferry, Thomas B. Whitbread, Stephen Kitay Orgel, Paul J. Alpers, Paul Bertram, Oswald Johnston, Thomas R. Edwards, Jr., William Youngren, G. Armour Craig, William R. Taylor, and Richard Poirier.

3. As this manuscript goes to the press, I am reading with admiration Russell B. Goodman, *American Philosophy and the Romantic Tradition,* in which he quotes Wittgenstein as saying: "I really want my copious punctuation marks to slow down the speed of reading. Because I should like to be read slowly. (As I myself read.)" The quotation is taken from *Culture and Value,* ed. G. H. von Wright and trans. Peter Winch (Chicago: Chicago University Press, 1980), 16.

WORKS CITED

Aaron, Daniel. *The Unwritten War: American Writers and the Civil War*. New York: Oxford University Press, 1975.

Ackroyd, Peter. *T. S. Eliot: A Life*. London: Hamish Hamilton, 1984.

Allen, Gay Wilson. *William James: A Biography*. New York: Viking, 1987.

Barzun, Jacques. *Darwin, Marx, Wagner: Critique of a Heritage*. Chicago: University of Chicago Press, 1941.

———. *A Stroll with William James*. London: University of Chicago Press, 1983.

Bataille, Georges. *Blue of Noon*. Tr. Harry Matthews. New York: Urizen Books, 1978.

———. *Visions of Excess: Selected Writings, 1927–1939*. Tr. Allan Stoekl et al. Minneapolis: University of Minnesota Press, 1985.

Bates, Milton. *Wallace Stevens: A Mythology of Self*. Berkeley: University of California Press, 1985.

Bersani, Leo. *The Culture of Redemption*. Cambridge: Harvard University Press, 1990.

Bishop, John Peale. "Homage to Hemingway." *After the Genteel Tradition: American Writers 1910–1930*. Ed. Malcolm Cowley. Carbondale: Southern Illinois University Press, 1964. 147–158.

Bloom, Harold. "Introduction." *Modern Critical Views: Gertrude Stein*. Ed. Harold Bloom. New York: Chelsea House, 1986. 1–6.

———. *The Poetics of Influence: New and Selected Criticism of Harold Bloom*. Ed. with an Introduction by John Hollander. New Haven: Henry R. Schwab, 1988.

———. *Wallace Stevens: The Poems of Our Climate*. Ithaca: Cornell University Press, 1976.

Bromwich, David. *A Choice of Inheritance: Self and Community from Edmund Burke to Robert Frost*. Cambridge: Harvard University Press, 1989.

———. "Stevens and the Idea of the Hero." *Raritan Quarterly*, 7:1 (1987), 1–27.

Brooks, Cleanth, and Robert Penn Warren, eds. *Understanding Poetry: An Anthology for College Students*. New York: Henry Holt, 1938.

Brower, Reuben A. *Alexander Pope: The Poetry of Allusion*. New York: Oxford University Press, 1968.

Brower, Reuben A., and Richard Poirier, eds. *In Defense of Reading*. New York: Dutton, 1962.

Burke, Kenneth. *Counter-Statement*. Third edition. Berkeley: University of California Press, 1968.

———. *A Grammar of Motives*. New York: Prentice-Hall, 1945.

———. *Language as Symbolic Action: Essays on Life, Literature, and Method*. Berkeley: University of California Press, 1966.

Burt, John. "Tyranny and the Public Sphere in *The Federalist*." *Raritan Quarterly*, forthcoming.

Cameron, Sharon. "Representing Grief: Emersons' 'Experience.' " *Representations*, 15 (1986), 15–41.

Carton, Evan. *The Rhetoric of American Romance*. Baltimore: Johns Hopkins University Press, 1985.

Cavell, Stanley. *In Quest of the Ordinary*. Chicago: University of Chicago Press, 1988.

———. *This New Yet Unapproachable America: Essays after Emerson after Wittgenstein*. Albuquerque: Living Batch Press, 1989.

Chapman, John Jay. "Emerson." *Selected Writings of John Jay Chapman*. Ed. Jacques Barzun. New York: Farrar, Straus, and Cudahy, 1957. 150–202.

Chessman, Harriet Scott. *The Public Is Invited to Dance: Representation, the Body, and Dialogue in Gertrude Stein*. Stanford: Stanford University Press, 1989.

Clausewitz, Carl von. *On War*. Ed. and tr. Michael Howard and Peter Paret. Princeton: Princeton University Press, 1976.

Cox, James. "R. W. Emerson: The Circles of the Eye." *Emerson: Prophecy, Metamorphosis, and Influence*. Ed. David Levin. New York: Columbia University Press, 1975. 57–82.

De Man, Paul. *Blindness and Insight: Essays in the Rhetoric of Contemporary Criticism*. New York: Oxford University Press, 1971.

———. "The Return to Philology." *TLS*, December 10, 1982, 1355–56.

Dewey, John. *Art as Experience*. New York: Minton, Balch and Co., 1934.

———. *Democracy and Education*. New York: Free Press, 1966.

———. "Ralph Waldo Emerson." *Characters and Events*, vol. I. Ed. John Dewey and Joseph Ratner. New York: Henry Holt, 1929. 69–77.

Dickinson, Emily. *The Complete Poems of Emily Dickinson*. 3 vols. Ed. Thomas H. Johnson. Boston: Little Brown, 1960.

Dimock, Wai-chee. *Empire for Liberty: Melville and the Poetics of Individualism*. Princeton: Princeton University Press, 1989.

Donadio, Stephen. "Emerson, Christian Identity, and the Dissolution of the Social Order." *Art, Politics, and Will: Essays in Honor of Lionel Trilling*. Ed. Quentin Anderson, Stephen Donadio, and Steven Marcus. New York: Basic Books, 1977. 99–123.

Eagleton, Terry. "Escape into the Ineffable." *TLS*, November 24, 1989, 1291–92.

Edel, Leon. *Henry James: The Conquest of London*. Philadelphia: Lippincott, 1963.

Edmundson, Mark. *Towards Reading Freud: Self-Creation in Milton, Wordsworth, Emerson, and Sigmund Freud*. Princeton: Princeton University Press, 1990.

Eliot, T. S. *Selected Prose of T. S. Eliot*. Ed. Frank Kermode. New York: Harcourt, Brace, Jovanovich, 1975.

Ellison, Julie. *Emerson's Romantic Style*. Princeton: Princeton University Press, 1984.

Emerson, Ralph Waldo. *Emerson in His Journals*. Sel. and ed. Joel Porte. Cambridge: Harvard University Press, 1982.

———. *Essays and Lectures*. Ed. Joel Porte. New York: The Library of America, 1983.

Feinstein, Howard M. *Becoming William James*. Ithaca: Cornell University Press, 1984.

Fisher, Philip. *Hard Facts: Setting and Form in the American Novel*. New York: Oxford University Press, 1985.

Frank, Joseph. "Spatial Form in American Literature." *Critiques and Essays in Criticism*. Ed. Robert W. Stallman. New York: The Ronald Press, 1949. 315–328.

Frost, Robert. *Complete Poems of Robert Frost*. New York: Holt, Rinehart and Winston, 1949.

———. *The Letters of Robert Frost to Louis Untermeyer*. New York: Holt, Rinehart and Winston, 1963.

———. *Selected Letters of Robert Frost*. Ed. Lawrance Thompson. New York: Holt, Rinehart and Winston, 1964.

———. *The Selected Prose of Robert Frost*. Ed. Hyde Cox and Edward Connery Lathem. New York: Collier, 1968.

Giamatti, A. Bartlett. *The University and the Public Interest*. New York: Atheneum, 1981.

Gilmore, Michael T. *American Romanticism and the Marketplace*. Chicago: University of Chicago Press, 1985.

Goodman, Russell B. *American Philsophy and the Romantic Tradition*. Cambridge: Cambridge University Press, 1990.

Grusin, Richard A. " 'Put God in Your Debt': Emerson's Economy of Expenditure." *PMLA*, 103:1 (1988), 35–44.

———. "Thoreau, Extravagance, and the Economy of Nature." Unpublished essay.

Hansen, Olaf. *Aesthetic Individualism and Practical Intellect: American Allegory in Emerson, Thoreau, Adams, and James*. Princeton: Princeton University Press, 1990.

Hobsbawm, Eric. "Introduction: Inventing Traditions." *The Invention of Tradition*. Ed. Eric Hobsbawm and Terence Ranger. Cambridge: Cambridge University Press, 1984. 1–14.

Hollander, John. *The Figure of Echo*. Berkeley: University of California Press, 1981.

————. *Melodious Guile: Fictive Patterns in Poetic Language.* New Haven: Yale University Press, 1988.

Horwitz, Howard. "The Standard Oil Trust as Emersonian Hero." *Raritan Quarterly,* 6:4 (1987), 97–119.

Howe, Irving. *The American Newness: Culture and Politics in the Age of Emerson.* Cambridge: Harvard University Press, 1986.

James, C. L. R. *Mariners, Renegades and Castaways.* London: Allison & Busby, 1985.

James, William. *The Selected Letters of William James.* Ed. Elizabeth Hardwick. New York: Farrar, Strauss, and Cudahy, 1980.

————. *The Works of William James.* Ed. Frederick Burkhardt, Fredson Bowers, et al. 16 vols. to date. Cambridge: Harvard University Press, 1975–.

Jay, Gregory S. *T. S. Eliot and the Poetics of Literary History.* Baton Rouge: Louisiana State University Press, 1983.

Jehlen, Myra. *American Incarnation: The Individual, the Nation, and the Continent.* Cambridge: Harvard University Press, 1986.

Kateb, George. "Individualism, Communitarianism, and Docility." *Social Research,* 56:4 (1989), 921–942.

————. "Thinking of Human Extinction (II): Emerson and Whitman." *Raritan Quarterly,* 6:3 (1987), 1–22.

Keach, William. *Shelley's Style.* New York: Metheun, 1984.

Kermode, Frank. *An Appetite for Poetry.* Cambridge: Harvard University Press, 1989.

————. *History and Value.* Oxford: Clarendon Press, 1988.

Kuklick, Bruce. *The Rise of American Philosophy: Cambridge, Massachusetts, 1860–1930.* New Haven: Yale University Press, 1977.

Lawrence, D. H. *Women in Love.* New York: Modern Library, 1937.

Lentricchia, Frank. *Criticism and Social Change.* Chicago: University of Chicago Press, 1983.

Levinson, Henry Samuel. "Santayana's Contribution to American Religious Philosophy." *Journal of the American Academy of Religion,* 52:1 (1984), 46–69.

Lopez, Michael. "Emerson's Rhetoric of War." *Prospects: An An-*

nual of American Cultural Studies. Ed. Jack Salzman. New York: Cambridge University Press, 1987. 293–320.

———. "Transcendental Failure: 'The Palace of Spiritual Power.'" *Emerson: Prospect and Retrospect.* Ed. Joel Porte. Cambridge: Harvard University Press, 1982. 121–153.

Marvell, Andrew. *Complete Poems.* Ed. Elizabeth Donno. New York: Penguin, 1977.

Matthiessen, F. O. *The Achievement of T. S. Eliot.* Third edition. New York: Oxford University Press, 1959.

———. *The James Family.* New York: Alfred A. Knopf, 1947.

McAleer, John. *Ralph Waldo Emerson: Days of Encounter.* Boston: Little, Brown, 1984.

Menand, Louis. *Discovering Modernism: T. S. Eliot and His Context.* New York: Oxford University Press, 1987.

Meyer, Steven. "Stein and Emerson." *Raritan Quarterly,* 10:2 (1990), 87–115.

Miller, J. Hillis. *The Linguistic Moment: From Wordsworth to Stevens.* Princeton: Princeton University Press, 1985.

Miller, Perry. *Errand into the Wilderness.* Cambridge: Harvard University Press, 1956.

Myers, Gerald E. *William James: His Life and Thought.* New Haven: Yale University Press, 1986.

Nietzsche, Friedrich. *The Gay Science.* Tr. Walter Kaufmann. New York: Vintage Books, 1974.

Packer, B. L. *Emerson's Fall: A New Interpretation of the Major Essays.* New York: Continuum, 1982.

Pease, Donald. *Visionary Compacts: American Renaissance Writings in Cultural Context.* Madison: University of Wisconsin Press, 1987.

Peirce, Charles S. *Selected Writings of Charles S. Peirce.* Ed. Philip P. Wiener. New York: Dover Publications, 1958.

Perry, Ralph Barton. *The Thought and Character of William James.* 2 vols. Boston: Little, Brown, 1935.

Poirier, Richard. "Afterword." *Robert Frost: The Work of Knowing.* New York: Oxford University Press, 1977. Reissue, Stanford: Stanford University Press, 1990. 315–338.

———. "Introduction." *Ralph Waldo Emerson.* Ed. Richard Poirier. New York: Oxford University Press, 1990. ix–xx.

———. "Pater, Joyce, Eliot." *James Joyce Quarterly* 26:1 (Fall 1988), 21–35.

———. *The Performing Self.* New York: Oxford University Press, 1971. Reissue, New Brunswick: Rutgers University Press, 1991.

———. *The Renewal of Literature.* New York: Random House, 1987.

———. "Robert Frost." *Voices and Visions: The Poet in America.* Ed. Helen Vendler. New York: Random House, 1987. 91–121.

———. *A World Elsewhere.* New York: Oxford University Press, 1966. Reissue, Madison: University of Wisconsin Press, 1985.

Porte, Joel. *Representative Man: Ralph Waldo Emerson in His Time.* New York: Oxford University Press, 1979.

Porter, David. *Emerson and Literary Change.* Cambridge: Harvard University Press, 1978.

Posnock, Ross. *The Trial of Curiosity: Henry James, William James, and the Challenge of Modernity.* Cambridge: Harvard University Press, 1991.

Rogin, Michael Paul. *Subversive Genealogy: The Politics and Art of Herman Melville.* Berkeley: University of California Press, 1985.

Rorty, Richard. *Consequences of Pragmatism (Essays: 1972–1980).* Minneapolis: University of Minnesota Press, 1982.

———. *Contingency, Irony, and Solidarity.* New York: Cambridge University Press, 1989.

———. "Just One More Species Doing Our Best." *London Review of Books* 13:14 (25 July 1991): 3–7.

Ruddick, Lisa. *Reading Gertrude Stein: Body, Text, Gnosis.* Ithaca: Cornell University Press, 1990.

Said, Edward. *Musical Elaborations.* New York: Columbia University Press, 1991.

———. *The World, the Text, and the Critic.* Cambridge: Harvard University Press, 1983.

Santayana, George. "Emerson's Poems Proclaim the Divinity of Nature, with Freedom as his Profoundest Ideal." *George Santayana's America: Essays on Literature and Culture*. Ed. James Ballowe. Urbana: University of Illinois Press, 1967. 84–96.

———. *Interpretations of Poetry and Religion*. New York: Scribner's, 1924.

———. *Persons and Places*. Ed. William G. Holzberger and Herman J. Saatkamp, Jr. Cambridge: MIT Press, 1986.

Stein, Gertrude. "Composition as Explanation." *Selected Writings of Gertrude Stein*. Ed. Carl Van Vechten. New York: Random House, 1946. 453–464.

———. *Everybody's Autobiography*. New York: Random House, 1937.

———. *The Geographical History of America or the Relation of Human Nature to the Human Mind*. New York: Random House, 1936.

———. *Stanzas in Meditation and Other Poems*. Preface by Donald Sutherland. New Haven: Yale University Press, 1956.

———. *Three Lives*. New York: Random House, 1936.

———. *The Yale Gertrude Stein*. Ed. Richard Kostelanetz. New Haven: Yale University Press, 1980.

Stevens, Wallace. *The Collected Poems of Wallace Stevens*. New York: Alfred A. Knopf, 1985.

———. *The Necessary Angel: Essays on Reality and the Imagination*. New York: Vintage, 1951.

———. *Opus Posthumous: Poems, Plays, Prose*. Ed. Milton J. Bates. New York: Afred A. Knopf, 1989.

Stimpson, Catharine. *Where the Meanings Are: Feminism and Cultural Spaces*. New York: Methuen, 1988.

Tanselle, G. Thomas. *A Rationale of Textual Criticism*. Philadelphia: University of Pennsylvania Press, 1989.

———. "Textual Criticism and Deconstruction." *Studies in Bibliography*, 43 (1990), 1–33.

Taylor, William R. *Cavalier and Yankee: The Old South and American National Character*. New York: George Braziller, 1961.

Thoreau, Henry David. *Journal*, volume 1: 1837–1844. Ed. Elizabeth Witherell. Princeton: Princeton University Press, 1981.

————. *A Week on the Concord and Merrimack Rivers, Walden, The Maine Woods, Cape Cod.* Ed. Robert F. Sayre. New York: The Library of America, 1985.

Tolman, George. *Mary Moody Emerson.* Privately printed, 1929.

Updike, John. "Emersonianism." *The New Yorker,* June 4, 1984, 122–132.

Vaihinger, Hans. *The Philosophy of As If: A System of the Theroetical, Practical, and Religious Fictions of Mankind.* Tr. C. K. Ogden. New York: Harcourt, Brace, 1924.

Vendler, Helen. "The Qualified Assertions of Wallace Stevens." *The Act of Mind.* Ed. Roy Harvey Pearce and J. Hillis Miller. Baltimore: Johns Hopkins University Press, 1965. 163–178.

Webb, Constance. *Richard Wright: A Biography.* New York: Putnam, 1968.

West, Cornel. *The American Evasion of Philosophy: A Genealogy of Pragmatism.* Madison: University of Wisconsin Press, 1989.

Whicher, Stephen. *Freedom and Fate: An Inner Biography of Ralph Waldo Emerson.* Philadelphia: University of Pennsylvania Press, 1953.

Wittgenstein, Ludwig. *Culture and Value.* Ed. G. H. von Wright. Tr. Peter Winch. Chicago: University of Chicago Press, 1980.

Wolff, Cynthia Griffin. *Emily Dickinson.* New York: Alfred A. Knopf, 1986.

Wordsworth, William. *Selected Poems and Prefaces by William Wordsworth.* Ed. Jack Stillinger. Boston: Houghton Mifflin, 1965.

INDEX

Aaron, Daniel, 203n16
Ackroyd, Peter, 200n14
Adams, Henry, 96
Alpers, Paul, 180, 209n2
American Scholar, The, 11
Amherst College, 174–175, 177, 180–181, 184–186, 188–190
Amherst Student, The, 186
Anderson, Quentin, 204n18
Anti-Imperialist League of New England, 114
Aquinas, Thomas, 184
Augustine, 133

Bacon, Francis, 133
Baird, Theodore, 180, 188, 190
Bakhtin, Mikhail, 190
Ballowe, James, 197n13
Barnes, Djuna, 187
Barthes, Roland, 187, 191
Bartlett, John, 137–138, 187
Barzun, Jacques, 195n2, 203n16
Bataille, Georges, 54, 59; *Visions of Excess* and *Blue of Noon,* 52–53
Bates, Milton: *Wallace Stevens: A Mythology of Self,* 159
Bell, Clive, 99, 202n10
Bergson, Henri, 66
Bersani, Leo: *The Culture of Redemption,* 53–54, 196n7
Bertram, Paul, 180, 209n2
Bishop, John Peale, 149
Blackmur, R. P., 10, 171, 184

Bloom, Harold, 101, 135, 149, 163–164, 186, 196n10, 202n11, 206n5
Bork, Robert, 11
Boydston, Jo Ann, 116
Bromwich, David: *A Choice of Inheritance,* 33, 203n15
Brooks, Cleanth: *Understanding Poetry,* 181, 184
Brooks, Peter, 180
Brooks, Van Wyck, 203n15
Brower, Reuben, 174, 177–184, 186, 188, 190–192, 209n2; *Alexander Pope: The Poetry of Allusion* and *In Defense of Reading,* 179
Burke, Kenneth, 10, 31, 96, 174, 177, 184, 189–191; *Language as Symbolic Action,* 90; "What Are the Signs of What," 102; *A Grammar of Motives,* 124, 189; *Counter-Statement,* 129
Burt, John, 206n4

Cambridge University, 177, 190–191
Cameron, Sharon, 198n5, 200n13
Carton, Evan, 200n1
Cavell, Stanley, 10, 173, 195n5, 198n6, 201n7
Chapman, John Jay: "Emerson," 6–7, 9–10, 113
Chessman, Harriet Scott, 206n3

221